Buzz about Bodacious! Woman

"This book has the power to change your life! In it's pages you will discover a strength you didn't know you had to fully be the woman you were meant to be – authentic, powerful, confident, and lovin' life!"

> Marta Brooks, co-author, *Your Leadership Legacy: The Difference You Make in People's Lives* of The Ken Blanchard Series

"What an eye-opener! I plan to start living bodaciously right away!"

> *Donna Bradshaw*

"I love how Mary says out loud what most of us only think! She let me see how attached I was to my inner good girl. And, she's right. I can't order off the kids' menu anymore. I'm ready to be bold, authentic, courageous and bodacious!"

> *Beth Dargis*

"*Bodacious! Woman* is the Games Mother Never Taught You for is millennium. Mary provides the GPS for both your personal and professional journey. Fasten your seat belt because your BoMo® is sure to be fast and furious!"

> *Cheryl Holmes*

"*Bodacious! Woman* is a blueprint for women who want to make the most out of their lives. I predict women everywhere will be tossing aside their good girl thoughts and jumping on the bodacious bandwagon for good!"

> *Terri Malloy*

"I really enjoyed your book and your lighthearted way of approaching everything. It is serious stuff but written in an easy to understand, light manner. Keep up the good work so we can change our ways....in a very positive way."

Shelly Bloom

"Wow, I never realized how much I was trying to be the good little girl. After reading *Bodacious! Woman* I am now more aware and able to correct this misconception I carried in my subconscious. Thank you, Mary Foley for changing my life, my career, and my relationships!"

Bernadette O'Dell

"I really enjoyed your book! Thanks for the fun and for reminder me to be less of a good girl and let my Bodacious Woman go!"

Sue Henthorne

"I loved your book! Best of all, it is good to know that I'm not alone being a good girl. Every woman should live their life by your Bodacious Woman Mantra!"

Bonnie Archer

"Mary offers encouragement to women in an unexpected but authentic way. She takes a very serious subject to a level that makes you smile."

Meryl Gorge

"Mary helps women to learn that being a good girl may be okay when you're 15, but when you're over 30 and working in a totally male environment like myself, that's when the woman inside us must take the courage to come out. She helps us understand how to become the women we want to be."

Virginia Vuturo, Italy

"Everyone needs to read Mary's book at least once. It will change your mind and your life!"

Kara Alford

"I finished *Bodacious! Woman* and LOVED it! It's filled with highlighted paragraphs and handwritten notes in the margins. Needless to say, it has inspired me and offered a ton of advice. I want to give it to every young woman I meet! Thanks again for your candor and for sharing your insights with the world!"

Allison Miller

"Your book is wonderful and so much fun to read. You have inspired me to take further steps on the path of bodaciousness (that word still makes me laugh, but I love it)."

Dusty Hooke

"You are such an exciting and interesting woman. I loved your book and think your advice is right on the money."

Elizabeth LeDoux

"My fiancé loves your book!"

Sean Smith

"Mary helps me remember how to go after what I want while staying focused and motivated. She is an inspiration to all women."

Deborah Traeger

"Your book has spoken to me in ways that you cannot imagine. It seems we have gotten to the same place…confident, having fun, not afraid and loving to get up in the morning. Thank you for putting it into words for me!"

Liz Mulholland

bodac!ous® woman

Bodacious! Woman: Outrageously In Charge of Your Life and Lovin' It
Copyright © 2007 Mary Foley

ISBN: 978-1-60037-275-9

Published by

MORGAN · JAMES
THE ENTREPRENEURIAL PUBLISHER
www.morganjamespublishing.com

Habitat
for Humanity®
Peninsula
Building Partner

Morgan James Publishing, LLC
1225 Franklin Ave. Ste 325
Garden City, NY 11530-1693
Toll Free: 800-485-4943
www.MorganJamesPublishing.com

bodacious® woman

*Outrageously in Charge
of Your Life and Lovin' It!*

Carol –
One Bodacious Woman!
Mary Foley

Mary Foley

Also by Mary Foley

Bodacious! Career: Outrageous Success for Working Women

Dedication

For my grandmother, "Spunky Ethel", whose bodacious,
loving spirit always shined through.

With a grandmother who nicknamed herself Spunky Ethel, I shouldn't be surprised that I wrote a book about being a Bodacious Woman. Spunky Ethel is my bodacious mother of origin and her legacy continues to this day through all of her grandchildren and great grandchildren.

I have very clear memories of my grandmother picking me up after school, and taking time to focus on me and my world. Sitting at the Roses discount store lunch counter, she taught me how a little love and chocolate cake can melt away the stresses of grade school. Later, as a teenager, I remember one hot summer day pulling up in front of her home to find her perched outside with a big smile on her face drinking a can of Pabst Blue Ribbon beer through a straw…with all the class and charm of her elegant dinner parties of years before. Then there was the time she put on head phones attached to a Sony Walkman. Her face lit up like a young girl who tasted fudge for the first time. She had spunk all right. She was living life on her own terms and loving every minute of it.

Spunky Ethel passed this independent thinking to my mom as well. I remember my mom telling me stories about how Grandma encouraged her to take solo bus trips downtown as a young teenager. My mom describes it as a wondrous, enlightening experience that grew her understanding of the world and her confidence. Like any parent, Spunky Ethel wanted her daughter to experience even more opportunity as a woman. Though Grandma was only able to attend a few years of college, she made sure her daughter would be able to graduate. I can only imagine how proud they both must have been when my mom received her diploma at graduation.

Of all the sayings Spunky Ethel favorite phrases sayings, the one that has stuck with me and meant more as the years go by is "This too shall pass."

She would often remind me of this truth when I was going through a tough time. I knew her life hadn't been easy. But, her gentle, warm smile was a testament that love and goodness ultimately prevail. Keep at it, I absorbed, and the difficulty will pass.

As I've earned my way to being an adolescent middle-age woman, I've come to appreciate Spunky Ethel's words in a whole new way. Not only will difficulties pass, but so will all the moments of joy, laughter, and the satisfaction of a job well done.

Spunky Ethel strove to make each moment we had together meaningful. Now in her advice, I hear this:

> "Embrace this life now while you have it.
> Be present.
> Be a full participant in your whole life.
> Live without regrets.
> You have this moment with your family and friends, live it.

You have this moment to go after your dreams, go for it.
You have this moment to make a difference, do it.
Don't worry about appearing too selfish or arrogant or bossy.
That ultimately doesn't matter.
What matters is that you lived truly lived every moment of
your life, that you felt every morsel, that you never gave up.
Because one day, this thing called life…this, too, shall pass."

And that is what I believe it really means to be a spunky, Bodacious Woman.

Here's to you Spunky Ethel!

Contents

About the Author

Mary Foley is a national thought leader for women, with a reputation for her spunk and experience.

Fresh out of college, Mary set aside her hard-earned engineering degree, to search for a career that she loved. She took a job as an $8 an hour customer service representative at a then-unknown computer startup America Online.

During AOL's hyper-growth, Mary was promoted four times, and she survived six layoffs, to become AOL's first head of Corporate Training, all while dealing with a difficult marriage. During those years she learned that being bold, positive, and courageous – bodacious – was the only way to thrive in today's world.

But her rapid rise through the ranks at AOL came to a sudden end, when she hit the glass ceiling. Not satisfied to settle, Mary made the bodacious decision to leave AOL and build her career another way. Through her writing, speaking, Bodacious Woman's Club (www.BodaciousWomensClub.com), Business Success For Her offerings (www.BusinessSuccessForHer.com), and more, Mary inspires women to be bodacious in life, career, and business.

Rather than CEO or President of her company Bodacious! Ventures, Mary proudly refers to herself as Woman in Charge. She holds a bachelor's in industrial engineering from Virginia Tech and a masters in organization development from Pepperdine University.

Preface

This book has the power to change your life! In its pages you will discover a strength you didn't know you had to fully be the woman you were meant to be – authentic, powerful, confident, and lovin' life! This is what my friend Mary Foley calls being bodacious! And I know you're going to enjoy yourself because Mary is, well frankly, a fun time. She tells it like it is in a very energetic, amusing way.

You see, I've known Mary Foley for almost 10 years, and I'll never forget the first time we met. I was in the lobby of the new AOL headquarters in Virginia gazing at the fabulous contemporary decor and wondering what the next few minutes would bring when I'd meet the new client who had hired my colleagues and I for a large training project. Suddenly from behind glass double doors, this five-foot-two-inch brunette spitfire came bopping out to greet us. I knew in an instant this woman was someone special.

I'm fortunate to have some clients who have become good friends. That's the case with Mary. Over the years, I've seen her rise in Corporate America, and I've watched this classy "good girl" chick turn into a powerful Bodacious Woman. And, let me tell you, it has been a wild ride!

Mary started at the ground level of one of the most influential Internet start-ups of our time. Nothing was predictable, everything was chaotic, and the faint-at-heart did not survive. On numerous, stress-filled occasions, I witnessed Mary provide unmistakable leadership with grace and poise. At her core was a passion for the company and its mission, as well as her desire for personal excellence.

In addition, I've watched her handle personal life trials that would bring most women to their knees. But not Mary. She courageously picked herself up, dusted herself off, and forged ahead. She continually chooses the path of growth and self-awareness through all of her experiences. Being a victim is not an option. She is bodaciousness personified.

In many ways, Mary has been the inspiration of my book, *Your Leadership Legacy: The Difference You Make in People's Lives.* Your legacy is the sum total of the positive difference you make in people's lives. Mary leaves her legacy everywhere she goes. When we would walk the AOL halls together, there hardly was a person who didn't know Mary and smiled as we passed. Today, she is building an even bigger legacy by helping women find their own bodacious spirit.

I am excited for you to begin your own bodacious, unforgettable journey! You truly can be the woman you want to be. And from this self-empowered place, you, too, can leave your own wonderful legacy – in your relationships, your family, your workplace, your business, and for us all.

Warmly,
Marta Brooks

co-author of *Your Leadership Legacy: The Difference You Make in People's Lives* of The Ken Blanchard Series

Acknowledgements

The more I write, the more I understand how every person in every moment of my life contributes to what I want to express and how I express it. To those whose paths I've had the privilege to cross, thank you.

Specifically, I thank the Bodacious Women included in this book who have inspired me by their personal BoMos® (bodacious moments) and words of advice about creating and living a life full of vigor and meaning: Ethel Somers, Queen Boudicca, Katharine Hepburn, Mae West, Kristi Lucariello, Lisa Earle McLeod, Jennifer Sterling, Christine Wall, Bethany Faulkner, Donna Wood, Deborah Young-Kroeger, Tiane Mitchell-Gordon, Nancy Regelin, Leslie Fagert, Ruth Cope, Tracy Kinard, Amy Cabellero, Diane Bradford, Alyson Skinner, Robin Sparks, and Lucy Stribley. Thanks to the many other Bodacious Women whose stories I was not able to include in this book, but whose encouragement of what I am doing is priceless and whose enthusiasm is contagious.

Thanks to David Hancock, founder of Morgan James Publishing (www.morganjamespublishing.com), for establishing a new, creative publishing model that will transform the publishing industry. I appreciate your entrepreneurial spirit and belief in me. Thanks to Ann Crawford for shepherding this book through the publishing process with such care.

Thanks to Angeline Robertson and Charley Foley of Scout Design (www.stateofscout.com). Your photography and graphic design truly capture the bodacious spirit in visual form. I'm lucky to have your expertise and I'm even luckier to have you in my family.

Last, but far from least, a huge thanks to my family and close friends for their unwavering, bodacious support, including Charles and Donna Foley, Leslie and Tim Fagert, Amy and Louie Cabellero, Charley Foley, Angeline Robertson, Marta Brooks, and the love of my life Bill Eastman. I am indebted to each of you.

And, thanks to the divine Creator, big kahuna, universal force, loving Lord, whom I call God. I don't know how it all works, but I do know the love, goodness, healing, and empowerment I've experienced comes from you.

1

I Want To Live Like My Nail Color

Wild berry. That's the name of my favorite nail color. To me it says fun, bold, sexy, and just simply makes my fingers and hands look so good. It's a funny name for a nail polish, but then so many women's cosmetics have funny names. There's Mango Spice lipstick, Roaring Red blush, and Whispering Mist eye shadow. Just saying these words makes me think of walking along the beach on a tropical island wearing a flowered sarong, matching top, and the perfect makeup to highlight my features against the setting sun. Oh, how the mind gets going! I so very much want to live like my nail color – **full-up on passion and feeling alive!** Take me away Wild Berry!

Now I *know* that painting my nails Wild Berry, or any color, for that matter, won't magically create this alive sensation. To feel that way has to come from within. Only after I've connected with, nurtured, and allowed myself to release my passion for life, can I truly be Wild Berry. Starting on the inside is the starting point for living up to my nail color.

But wait! What if you don't wear nail color? Many women I know prefer to have their nails "au naturel". Their nails are trim, buffed, and clean, but they don't sport a bright red or hot pink color. Maybe they have a clear coat, but that's it. Not a problem. Rather than being plain, I like to think of natural nails as being authentic. Living like your nail color is an attitude; it's a perspective on life. Wearing them in their natural mode says you dare to be your natural self.

Who knew there was so much to learn from a nail color? Who knew that when I started my young-adult life as an $8 an hour customer service rep at America Online, I would rise through the ranks, get married along the way, and discover in myself the desire to be much more like my nail color than I ever expected? My internal good girl was aghast! But my inner Bodacious Woman was starting to push her way to the forefront. Good thing, too, because personally and professionally, life would knock me around a bit and test just how much I wanted to be wild about taking care of myself as well as my future.

And, I'm not alone. Many women struggle to feel good about themselves and their lives. Perhaps you're one of them. You've wanted to feel like your nail color but you've had fears or guilt or pressure in your life to stay put and not cause waves. Been there, done that, and it's not a fun time! In my own struggle, there were times when I wanted to feel like Wild Berry but I felt more like Wet Leaves. But, in time, I found another way, a way that affirmed my existing internal strength and enabled me to get stronger, wiser, healthier, and be a whole lot more fun! I call it the Bodacious Way.

It All Starts with One Bodacious Move

Discovering the Bodacious Way happens one step at a time. And I didn't even know I was taking one! You might be wondering how

I found another way, a way that affirmed my existing internal strength and enabled me to get **stronger**, *wiser*, *healthier*, and be *a whole lot more fun!*

I call it the

Bodacious Way.

I started working at AOL for $8 an hour as a customer service rep and worked my way up to be head of corporate training for the entire company. After reading dozens of books for women about how to carve out a career, you might be thinking that I had a detailed, step-by-step plan that I executed without flaw. And you would be right. You'd also be right in saying that I'm currently 25 years old and used to be a blonde – just like my photo on the cover. I don't think so!

The truth is I took the $8 an hour gig because I had just graduated from college with an engineering degree and needed a job. Now I know for sure what you're thinking. Mary, if you're smart enough to get your engineering degree, aren't you clued in to the fact that you can make more than 8 bucks an hour with that education? Of course, you're right! Here's the deal: By the time I'd finished my degree, I realized something very profound and life altering. Are you sitting down? I realized I didn't want to be an engineer! (Gasp! I know right now I'm striking fear into any parent whose daughter is in engineering school, or any profession for that matter.) The thought of doing that kind of work day after day for rest of my life made me depressed. It felt like a sentence, and I hadn't even started!

One thing I knew for sure was that I had been launched from the nest – and I had bills to pay. So I decided to move from my small hometown of Williamsburg, Virginia, to the big city of Washington, D.C., to get a job, *any job*, to pay the bills. That's when I saw an ad in the *Washington Post* from some small, unknown computer company. They were looking for people to help their customers get online, whatever that was. Hey, it was 1988! I had no clue what online meant then!

I'd had a few retail jobs in high school and worked with computers in college, so I knew I was more than qualified. Fortunately, they did, too, and offered me the job. So, in July of 1988, I officially started my career with the idea that I'd do this customer service gig for about three months and then hitch a ride with a bigger company with more opportunity and better pay.

What I didn't recognize then was that I was making one of my first bodacious moves. **I was searching for something I cared about, something I loved.** My parents just thought I was nuts for not using my engineering education. But then again, I was young and idealistic and primed for being corrupted by AOL. The people at AOL had passion for what they were doing, and their enthusiasm was contagious. When you're in that kind of environment, it's not idealistic, it's real. You're motivated, you're pumped; you care about getting up every day and doing your part. It corrupts you because you don't want to settle for anything less. It was certainly a Wild Berry experience!

I loved the company, the people, and the energy, and ended up staying much longer than I ever anticipated. Through company financial ups and downs, six layoffs, working my way up the ranks, having a ball, and stretching myself for everything I was worth, three months turned into ten and a half years. Ten and a half amazing, challenging, delightful, formative years that ended a bit unexpectedly. At first, it was a hard pill to swallow. But the lessons gained were invaluable.

I'd come to a place I'd only heard of – one I thought would never happen to me – the glass ceiling.

Going to Work Without Your Pants Is A Career-Limiting Move, Or Is It?

You see, for all of my accomplishments and recognition at AOL, there came a time when I was struggling to get my manager to view me as a young woman who was ready for more responsibility, ready for a promotion. I had many discussions with him about this, but alas, he simply wasn't buying. I'd come to a place I'd only heard of – one I thought would never happen to me – the glass ceiling.

The glass ceiling on the corporate ladder means you can clearly see the way up, but there's only so far you can go. It felt like an invisible force field was keeping me down. And I'm now convinced it was put there by guys who watched too much *Star Trek*! When I was growing up in the 1970s, I would watch *Star Trek* because I thought Captain Kirk was oh, so cute. Obviously I was paying attention to the wrong thing! I should have been learning a technical thing or two from Scotty, the engineer, about invisible force fields!

Meet Bodacious Woman Mae West

When I ask, as I often do, what comes to mind when someone hears the word "bodacious," sometimes I get the instant response of "Mae West!" The immediate reason is because of her ta-ta's, but it doesn't stop there. She's also thought of as witty, gutsy, and fun. And for good reason. She's known for such immortal lines as, "Too much of a good thing is wonderful," and "I used to be Snow White, but I drifted."

It all started in Brooklyn, New York, when West was born in 1893. She was already a Vaudeville child star by age six. As she grew older, she wrote and performed plays, including one called *Sex* which was apparently quite scandalous, and for which she was arrested. That was in 1926; I wonder if it would be a big deal today. Chances are it wasn't more explicit than the Broadway and movie hit, *Chicago*. But Mae kept on going. In 1932, she wrote and performed in her best-known film, *She Done Him Wrong*. Apparently her audience liked it, but the then-current political and religious climate saw her open sexuality as a threat to morality. Each film thereafter was increasingly censored. As a result, her provocative style of humor became so diluted that West abandoned her movie career.

By the time she retreated from the silver screen, she had made nine movies, five with writer's credits. Her popularity also raised enough money to bring the near-bankrupt studio, Paramount, into the black. One biographer had this to say about this Bodacious Woman: "Many movie comediennes have come along after Mae West, but none have equaled her talent. Mae was whimsical, sexy, irreverent and ahead of her time. She was an actor, dancer, writer, producer, and director at a time when women rarely had jobs outside of the home. Her risqué delivery of such immortal lines as 'Come up and see me sometime' and 'Is that a gun in your pocket or are you just happy to see me?' are as tantalizing today as when they were first heard over sixty years ago." West died in 1980.

I decided that instead of bumping my head against the glass ceiling, I'd take a different route to grow my career. I decided to apply to grad school. But I didn't want my reputation at work to falter while waiting to find out if I was accepted. As it turned out, I took on the biggest management training project done to date at the company. I was responsible for making sure over 400 managers went through four new training programs in four months! The pressure was on more than ever.

One day, I was on a tight deadline. That morning I had several back-to-back meetings with key people to make some final decisions for the training design, which had to be done a few days later. It had taken nearly an act of God to get these people together because of their schedules, but I was determined we'd find time to meet.

I decided to get up early to work out and relieve some of the stress I was accumulating around this all-important initiative. The alarm went off, the workout clothes went on, and I hurriedly put my office clothes into a gym bag and headed out to the fitness center at AOL. Running on the treadmill and pumping iron on the weight machines was just what I needed to relax.

Later in the locker room after my shower, I stood with a towel wrapped around me, my hair dripping wet and suddenly realized I had a big, big problem. A monumental crisis. I HAD NO PANTS!

Oh, those pants were there when I mentally reviewed the checklist on my drive to work. But, somehow those pants never made it from lying on my bed into my gym bag. And, here I was, with only 45 minutes before my first important meeting of the day!

Where I lived in the Washington, D.C. area you can't get anywhere in 45 minutes, let alone to drive home and back to shower and change. But if I cancelled any of my meetings, getting these folks together again would require more divine intervention!

What was I going to do? Whatever it was, I had to make a decision quick! I took a deep breath and decided, Okay, that's it! I'm going to these meetings in the only clothes I've got – my skin-hugging Lycra shorts and T-shirt! Ugh! Why did I succumb to the fitness fashion of tight shorts? I know I was feeling proud of how I'd made such fitness progress, but that was not helping me now. Then I caught myself in the mirror. Where did those dimples on my thighs come from? They weren't there yesterday!

Fortunately, in that moment I had a revelation, something that just might make my clothing choice less noticeable. I remembered that AOL had a casual dress code! Yeah, and on top of all that, my T-shirt looked like a team jersey with a big XXL across the front. Then I noticed that my ID badge around my neck almost looked like a whistle. I mean, I am like a team coach, right, being that I'm the head of corporate training? Right! So, with only 30 minutes left, I got dressed and ran to my first meeting. As I walked through the door, I proudly announced, "Your head trainer and coach is here, so let's get started!" They laughed, I laughed, and, most importantly, I left with the decisions I needed to meet my deadline.

This happened at the first, second, and third meetings until I had a break in my day when I decided to go home to change. And, while I was at home changing out of my head trainer disguise, I honestly still felt a little stupid that I had forgotten my pants. But **I also had a grin on my face because I hadn't let that become a barrier** to troopin' on with my morning and making it successful. At that moment, I put my hands on my hips and announced to myself in the bathroom mirror, Mary, that's just a little bit of bodaciousness!

The Bodacious Queen

Bodacious. Whenever I say that word it always cracks a smile on another person's face.

What comes to mind when you think of the word bodacious? I love asking that question! I've heard everything – wild, colorful, spontaneous, energetic, strong, fearless, courageous, assertive, open, free, gutsy, tenacious, confident, positive, etc. And the one many people think but don't usually say – ta-ta's. Other than the busty reference, when you look up bodacious in the dictionary (the online version of *Merriam-Webster*, of course) you will find similar descriptors like *outright, unmistakable, remarkable,* and *noteworthy*. In addition to having a gutsy connotation, the word bodacious is just downright fun to say! You can say it fast or you can say it slow, and either way it just rolls off your tongue like *buttah*!

No one's certain where the term *bodacious* comes from, but in my love for understanding bodacious, I ran across an ancient Bodacious Woman, who, in my heart-of-hearts, I believe, had something to do with it. The common belief is that bodacious started as a term in the southern United States, and is the combination of the words *bold* and *audacious*. Okay, sounds reasonable. Not exciting, but reasonable. Then someone asked me if I'd heard of Queen Boudicca (pronounced bow-da-see-ah). Queen who? Obviously, this was not covered in my engineering education. Her name was so similar to the spelling of bodacious that I had to find out!

And was I a happy camper with what I found! Now follow me on this one. It turns out Queen Boudicca was the wife of King Prasutagus (pronounce his name any way you want!) of the Iceni, a British tribe that lived near the modern town of Colchester in England during the time of the Roman Emperor Nero.

BoMo®:

It's a moment when you know you have the courage to be bold,

when you take a risk,

when you stand up for yourself.

(a bodacious moment)

BoMos® are one of the most rewarding things about being a Bodacious Woman.

My Own Set of Balls

Bodacious Woman Kristi Lucariello

One of my BoMos® was almost 20 years ago, and I remember it like it was yesterday. Alone, in my Ford Mustang, I drove cross country from a small Midwest town to Phoenix, Arizona. My first week, I was invited to attend a women's networking group where the speaker encouraged us to be more bold and take risks. You know, just like men. (Obviously she was a very bodacious speaker!)

To help us remember our masculine energy, she gave each of us two small fuzzy balls. We could no longer avoid living our greatness because now we had our own set of balls!

That afternoon, I had an interview with a financial institution. I felt the position was exactly what I was looking for. The hiring manager said there were several other candidates and that he would contact me next week. He didn't know that I had a job offer from another company, which I needed to accept or decline the following morning. With my newly acquired balls in my pocket, I boldly told him that I couldn't wait until next week, that I knew I was the right person for job, and that if he wanted me to work with him, I needed to know first thing in the morning.

By the time I got back to my apartment, there was a phone message offering me the job! For seven years, I had an extremely exciting and successful career there. And, later that same day, I met my future husband. We've been married for over 18 years!

When the king died, the Roman government decided to seize the queen's wealth. Queen Boudicca protested and the Roman soldiers whipped her and raped her two daughters. Needless to say, she was ticked. She wasn't about to take this treatment! So she called her tribe together and led a rebellion against the Romans, you know, the most powerful people on the earth at the time.

Now let me stop right here and say that when the Queen Bee decided to lead the rebellion, she experienced what I call a BoMo®, a Bodacious Moment. It's a moment when you know you have the courage to be bold, when you take a risk, when you stand up for yourself.

One of the most rewarding things about being Bodacious Women is having BoMos®. I have them myself and love watching others do the same. That's why throughout this book, you'll see BoMos® from Bodacious Women just like you and me. You don't have to be a historical queen to have BoMos®, you just have to be alert to when these moments show up for you, then have a mini-triumph!

I've highlighted these BoMos® with a sunglasses icon, because usually, in those moments, we feel hip, cool, and refreshed inside. So, whenever you see this icon, take a moment to read this Bodacious Woman's Bodacious Moment of personal victory and silently celebrate with her once again! You just might relate to exactly what she went through.

In addition to BoMos® in forthcoming chapters, I've also included advice from everyday Bodacious Women. Look for the lips icon, the quintessential symbol of a woman: affection and support. These nuggets are worth reading in and of themselves!

Now back to the queen's story. From what I learned, it doesn't sound like Queen Boudicca was a woman to be reckoned with, either. She's described as "terrifying of aspect, with a harsh voice, a great mass of bright red hair (who) grasped a spear to strike fear into all who watched her." The Romans also were thrown off by the fact that she was a woman; the idea of female leadership was strange to them. She decided to throw them off further by going into battle bare-breasted (perhaps this is the origin of the ta-ta's association).

As a result of her revolts, the cities of London, Colchester, and St. Albans burned to the ground. Author Gary Sutton, who researched Queen Boudicca, says that "Professors, authorities and experts dismissed Boudicca as a myth until 1919. In that year, archeologists digging under London, St. Albans, and Colchester found thick layers of ash thirteen feet down. That depth matches Boudicca's time. It took nearly two thousand years, but she finally got into the history books. Those old 'myths' also reported that Boudicca's revolt killed 80,000 Romans. If true, she outperformed Spartacus and Hannibal." Basically, Charlie's Angels have nothing on this woman. She died in A.D. 60. Today, there's a bronze statue of Queen Boudicca in London, where she's revered as a symbol of British freedom.

Was this Queen Bodacious or what? Talk about tremendous courage! I don't know if hundreds of years later some Pilgrims brought the Boudicca story to the New World, which gave birth to our modern-day term bodacious, but I'd certainly like to think so.

Two of my other favorite influential Bodacious Women in history are Mae West and Katharine Hepburn. Be inspired by their stories by checking out the related sidebars in this chapter. Also, flip to the dedication page at front of this book and be encouraged by a Bodacious Woman in my own family tree, my grandmother Spunky Ethel.

Meet Bodacious Woman Katharine Hepburn

In the summer of 2003, we lost actress Katharine Hepburn's physical presence, but her spirit lives on in her movies and in the way she lived her life. Here are three gems from this Bodacious Woman's life that all women can learn from.

First and foremost, Hepburn focused on succeeding, not on the fact that most of the players in the movie industry were men. She acknowledged that it was very much a man's world, especially in the 1930s and 1940s when she started. But, she didn't limit herself because of it. Putting her primary energy into her craft, she said, "I always considered myself pretty bright with a good sense of what worked with an audience and what didn't. So I would speak my mind. But, after I had my say, I knew to shut up. I listened to the good strong directors...and learned from them." It showed. She kept getting better and her long list of movies and plays proved she refused to accept a short acting career based on youth and beauty.

Secondly, Hepburn never relinquished her femininity. One of her best-known films is *Woman of the Year*, where she met and fell in love with co-star Spencer Tracy. Hepburn projected her own thoughts into her character Tess Harding. She said that "Tess was not trying to be a man. She was someone like me...working in a man's world, succeeding. And like my mother – who held her own with men without compromising her femininity." Katharine described how her mother would lobby leaders and politicians about a woman's right to vote while asking how they would like their tea. Her mother not only refused to sacrifice her femininity, she used it to get an ear in ways that men could not.

Lastly, Hepburn always expected to work hard for her success, and she kept at it. She rose to movie stardom quickly, but found the status hard to maintain. She then fell into a period of what she called *disaster* films and had become a *joke* in Broadway. She was tagged *box office poison* when several back-to-back films did not do well. Even well-known films such as *Bringing Up Baby* did not produce big profits. At the same time, her beloved family home in Connecticut was washed out by a hurricane. Still, she didn't give up. She kept searching for parts and worked hard to change the tide. Finally, she broke through with the hit *The Philadelphia Story*.

Katharine Hepburn embodied the modern woman. She acknowledged the challenges and dynamics of working with men, but assumed she could succeed. She maintained her femininity and used it to help her. She expected to work hard for success, and did. These are three bodacious characteristics of a most Bodacious Woman. May we learn from her example; may she rest in peace.

A Personal Rallying Cry

Being bodacious became a personal rallying cry during my years at AOL. You see, in the midst of the pressures, loving my job and experiencing the glass ceiling, I learned something unexpected and something that took courage to face. I learned that being a good girl wasn't good enough.

Like so many women, I had been raised a good girl, someone who was so oriented toward being nice and thinking of what others wanted that I didn't know what I wanted for myself. And goodness knows it would be selfish to ask! I was such a people pleaser that when people were critical, I assumed it was something I did that made them angry. It was all about me, but in an unhealthy way.

Being a Bodacious Mom

Bodacious Woman **Lisa Earle McLeod**, author of the hilarious book *Forget Perfect*

I always thought being a mom meant conservative clothes, lots of cooking and cleaning, and no life of your own. And now that I'm a mother I realize that is, of course, correct. But there's also a fun part a lot of people don't tell you about.

One particular BoMo® happened when I was on vacation with my kids. Actually I was dragging them to a conference where I was asked to speak. But my speech would only take two hours, and the rest of the weekend we had a free condo at the beach.

The trip began with a long boring car ride. I was by myself with no hubby or friend to take over the driving or entertainment duties, so when the kids got bored, I resorted to throwing a bag of junk food over the seat every 15 minutes to keep them quiet, while snagging large handfuls for myself. We were all on a sugar-induced high when we entered a radio dead zone. I realized all I had was an old cassette of show tunes. Beggars can't be choosers, so I popped it in and we spent the remainder of the trip belting out Broadway's best at the top of our lungs. When the kids didn't know all the words, we made some up, including a lovely rendition of "come to our messy car" sung to the tune of *Cabaret*.

It wasn't scaling a mountain or taking on the big boys in a boardroom, but I like to think a Bodacious Woman knows how to make the most of every moment, especially when she's sharing it with overtired toddlers fighting over *Cheetos*.

bodacious®

{ The courage to be in charge of your life. }

As I gained more responsibility and rose through the ranks of AOL, I noticed that being a good girl wasn't working. I was still friendly to others, and I strove to be competent, but I was challenged more than ever to give my opinion at meetings or to talk one-on-one with someone who was being difficult.

Then my co-worker Tiane Mitchell-Gordon gave me the book *The Bodacious Book of Succulence* by SARK. She saw me struggling and thought the author's words might help. She was right, but it was actually one word in the title that stood out. It was a word I hadn't heard in a long time, and immediately, it made me grin. No big punch line here – obviously that word was bodacious. Right then I knew that being bodacious was the alternative to being a good girl that I needed.

Being bodacious gives me courage to make choices, small and large, that are *good for me*. Being bodacious gives me the courage to take risks. And on hard days, being bodacious gives me the courage to put one foot in front of the other.

I've come up with my own definition of bodacious: The courage to be in charge of your life. Being in charge of your life starts with being authentic with yourself, about who you are and what you want. It then takes courage to follow through. Courage is something that never goes out of style because contrary to what the media says, ultimately life isn't a fashion show. Shocker, I know.

Yep, life is hard work. Keeping at it, picking yourself up when circumstances stare you down, looking within to ponder what's there for you to learn, feeling the joy of what's good in your life, all of this and more simply takes guts. It takes being bodacious!

Live Life as an Exclamation, Not an Explanation!

The great part is that we all have a little bodaciousness already going for us! Seriously. It's just a matter of deciding to recognize it, nurture it, and let it grow. I can show you how with my Bodacious Woman Mantra. It's just so much easier to wrap our hearts and minds around an idea when we have it laid out for us in uncomplicated terms. I mean, who needs fussy? My Bodacious Woman Mantra will show you the Bodacious Way.

What I've learned in my bodacious journey is that Bodacious Women live their lives as an exclamation, not an explanation. Bodacious Women are in charge of their lives and don't feel the need to give courtroom justification as to why they act the way they do.

How outrageous! That's how it may seem to others and even to you at times. But, don't worry. Whether you're an introvert or an extrovert, knowing that you're acting in a way that's personally

DIAGRAM OF A *Bodacious* WOMAN

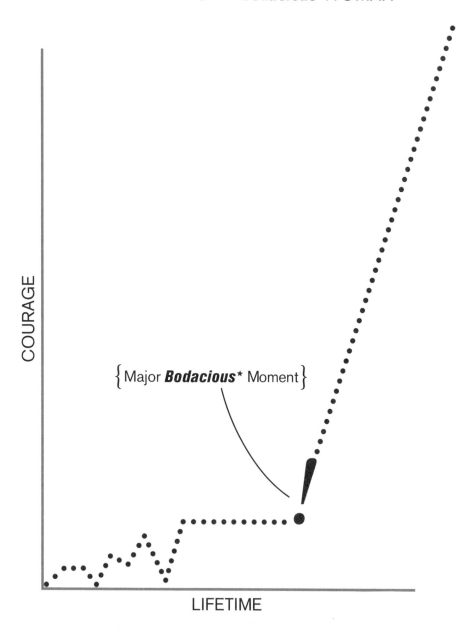

COURAGE

{ Major *Bodacious** Moment }

LIFETIME

Bodacious: the courage to be in charge of your life

empowering, knowing that you're having a BoMo....well, it's so worth it. And in that moment, you're like a walking exclamation point!

On your journey there's one thing I bet my bodacious booties on that you're going to have to get over, around, or through to follow the Bodacious Woman Mantra and be the Bodacious Woman you want to be. I know I did. You're going to have to deal with your internal good girl once and for all. Being a good girl isn't good enough.

Right now that may sound a bit harsh, but stay with me on this. Remember, it's bodacious we're shooting for, not *bad*acious. Even if you feel pretty good about yourself, you might be surprised where the good girl is still hanging out in your life. I was absolutely blindsided! But the good news is that I found my bodacious sunglasses, had a few powerful BoMos®, and came out a more authentic, powerful Bodacious Woman. I'm certain you can, too!

Remember, it's *bodacious* we're shooting for, not *badacious*.

Exclamation Points

! Decide to live like your nail color - full up on passion and fully alive - even if your nails are "au naturel".

! Bodacious means to have the courage to be in charge of your life. Think Queen Boudicca, Mae West, or Katharine Hepburn – or you!

! Notice the BoMos® in your life, those bodacious moments when you are bold, when you take a risk, or when you stand up for yourself. Give yourself an internal high-five!

2

Being A Good Girl Isn't Good Enough

In striving to live your life as an exclamation (as well as living up to your nail color), it's likely you're going to have to part ways with one of your dear childhood friends. This person may have served you in a number of ways as a young child, but no longer supports you much as an adult. Think I've looked up your history in the where-are-they-now high-school yearbook web sites? Naah. My experience tells me this childhood friend is someone you know very well. She's been with you through thick and thin. And guess what? She's your internal good girl.

The dilemma is that she's no longer cutting it. Call me Lucy the 5¢ psychiatrist on this one, but my personal experience has taught me that being a good girl is no longer good enough for today's woman in today's world. Time to say ciao to your inner good girl and hello to your inner Bodacious Woman!

You've Got "Good" and You've Got "Girl"

What do I mean by good girl? Well, let's start with the fact that she's *good* and she's a *girl*. By being good, she's thoughtful toward others, considers their needs before her own, works hard at the office and at home, is extremely responsible, and never, ever wants to hurt anyone's feelings. These seem like admirable qualities, but in the process of pleasing everyone else first, she'll sacrifice her own needs. She'll keep taking on more responsibility, and people will keep giving her more because she can't say no. The result? She'll hide her feelings and let others walk all over her in order to avoid conflict. Ultimately, people pleasing will work against her.

Thinking of yourself as a *girl* only diminishes your personal power.

She might be called *nice*, which was the kiss of death when young sorority recruits were being discussed during my college days. *Nice* said nothing about what the young woman was really like. *Nice* said vanilla. Imagine if a woman was described as chocolate raspberry, strawberry supreme, or rainbow sherbet. Now *that* would have said something about her! Come to think of it, choosing an ice cream flavor was my predecessor to choosing a nail color. Being a bit older now, I have to watch my calories!

The other part about being a good girl that I'm not crazy about is being referred to as a *girl*. I'll go to Las Vegas right now and put $10,000 down on a bet that you're over 18 years old. You are no longer a girl. You're an adult woman! Even the state says so. **You can't order off the kids menu any more.**

My First Client

Bodacious Woman Jennifer Sterling

The hardest part for a brand new, self-employed designer is landing that first client. Ten years ago, I walked into a small audio/video repair shop that was in a building near where I worked. I told the owner that unless his wife designed his store sign, I could do it better. I don't know what came over me, but it worked! He was so shocked by my boldness that he said yes. My first client!

THE
"WHO ARE YOU CALLING A *GIRL*?"
EXPERIMENT

Conduct this mini-experiment: For the next seven days, only use the term "woman" when talking about yourself or other adult females.

MONDAY ~~||||~~ ~~||||~~ ~~||||~~ ||

TUESDAY ~~||||~~ ~~||||~~ ~~||||~~

WEDNESDAY ~~||||~~ ~~||||~~ ||

THURSDAY ~~||||~~ ~~||||~~

FRIDAY ~~||||~~ ~~||||~~ ~~||||~~ ~~||||~~ ||||

(such a bodacious day!)

SATURDAY ~~||||~~ ~~||||~~

SUNDAY ~~||||~~ ||||

You might be a scared woman, a worried woman, or an insecure woman at times, but you're still a woman. So, embrace the moniker! You might also be a confident woman, an authentic woman, a loving woman, and a Bodacious Woman. Thinking of yourself as a girl only diminishes your personal power.

I'm not trying to be obsessive or defensive about a single word. It's just that language is much more powerful than we often realize. The words we use send messages to both ourselves and others about who we are and how we see ourselves. Behaviors that support these beliefs tend to follow.

Still not convinced? Conduct this mini-experiment: For the next seven days, only use the term *woman* when talking about yourself or other adult females. Notice how many times you catch yourself making a correction. Notice how using the term *woman* reflects how you think of yourself and others. As a manager at AOL, I deliberately decided to greet groups of women in the lunchroom or otherwise as *ladies*. My simple act of esteeming them made them smile, and I noticed how they sat straighter and esteemed themselves. I still address groups of women like this today, though now I call them Bodacious Women instead!

You Really Should

Good girls often don't feel good enough because there's always something they feel they should or have to or had better do. My good girl alert always goes off when I hear someone start a sentence with the words I *should*...I often ask, **"Is that something you *should* do or is that something you *want* to do?" There's a big difference.** Good girls do a lot of things out of a sense of obligation or duty. Not much energy in that!

SHOULD vs. WANT

97   **3**

But if that's where you're at right now, then you really *should* become a Bodacious Woman. And the first thing you *should* do is to deep six the *shoulds* from your life and only do those things that you want to do. Even taxing activities for fulfilling a responsibility (like parenting or delivering a big presentation at work) can be reframed as something you *want* to do for a greater end result. You *should* do that, *shouldn't* you?

When I was a child, I was very compliant. I followed all the rules and respected authority and leadership like I should have, or at least those in authority easily intimidated me so much that I was afraid to step out of line. Rules served me well as a little girl. They protected me and taught me discipline when I was developing into an adult who was expected to take care of herself. Now as that adult, I look at rules in a whole new light. Instead of simply dutifully following rules, I consider their relevance to my own situation and decide if they serve my intention. Living bodaciously, I find myself following or breaking rules as I deem necessary.

What are the rules anyway and who came up with them? It seems so many rules aren't real rules at all, just common norms of behavior

Life On My Own

Bodacious Woman **Christine Wall**

When I graduated from college, I had everything planned out. I was engaged to be married to a man who was everything my parents and I ever wanted, including being an investment banker and on his way to attending a prestigious business school. When I got my first job, I quickly realized that I had no real identity of my own; it was all tied to my fiancé. I found work to be very satisfying. And, the more successful I became, the more problems I had with my fiancé. I eventually called off the wedding and explored life on my own. At first it was scary! I traveled to Europe on my own and continued to be successful in my career. Today, I'm a top sales person, have a wonderful husband who supports me, two wonderful kids, and supportive family and friends.

that fall into the category of everyone does it that way. Or worse, rules that tell you to play small, to wait until everyone has stopped speaking before you can open your mouth, to wait to be acknowledged or called upon. Or take what you've been given, be grateful, and expect no more. When I was a little good girl in elementary school, I was convinced there were entire families who would sit at the kitchen table with their peanut butter and jelly sandwiches and milk, quietly waiting until the stroke of noon to eat lunch, the official, preordained lunch start time.

The universe is not going to give you a noogie just because you leave the shopping cart in the middle of the parking lot, take the biggest piece, change your assigned seat to a more comfortable one after the plane has taken off, request a better table at a restaurant, ask for a discount, or use one job offer to leverage an improved offer from a competitor. You can do these things. In fact, perhaps you *should*.

I'll Be Just Fine

Being a good girl isn't good enough because it doesn't equip us to manage, let alone thrive, on the constant change of today's world. Being a good girl is a way to avoid unpleasant realities. For example, a good girl might decide not to be involved in the financial side of her life because someone else is taking care of that. But deep down, she's paralyzed by the thought of making financial decisions on her own. A good girl may be thrilled that she's no longer single and has someone to share her life, when in reality, she's petrified of ever dealing with the dating scene again. Another good girl may be excited about finally being a mom, is anticipating the wonder years ahead, but can't even think about the possibility of carrying the parenting responsibility alone.

You Cannot Control Me

Very Young Bodacious Woman Bethany Faulkner

I'm five years old, and recently I was at the playground rocking back and forth on the toy horse named Phil. It was fun, and so was my playmate. But, then my friend started saying Phil needed to be fed and that I had to get off. He kept repeating this over and over again. I knew he just wanted to ride on Phil and make me get off. I stopped rocking, looked right at him and declared, "You cannot control me!" He stood there staring with no words coming out of his mouth. My mom said that what I did was bodacious; I just knew he wasn't treating me right.

Good girls tend to choose to believe life will be just fine. But losing financial, emotional, parenting support, and a whole bunch of other stuff *does* happen – to good girls and Bodacious Women alike. It's just that Bodacious Women have different coping strategies.

The main good girl strategy is to please others, and be liked by everyone so someone will take care of you so you won't get hurt. The focus of this strategy is on other people. The problem is that this leaves you open to letting others define who you are, how you feel, and where you're going. You have to depend on other people, who may or may not be there for you. Then, when your so-called supporters let you down, you're crushed, left holding the bag, with no one to blame really but yourself for letting others have control. It's then you may finally come to realize you need to look after you.

I Remember When

My heart aches for the good girls because when this kind of pain happens, it's a tough place to be. I remember when my good girl world came crashing down because of my marriage. Things got so bad at my lowest point that I didn't care much if I lived or died. I never imagined feeling like a living corpse, functioning well on the outside while my spirit was dying on the inside from a critical, abusive relationship. I felt trapped in my good girl ways, believing that if I just loved my husband enough, he wouldn't feel the need to hit me or call me names or be just plain mean.

My good girl was afraid to confront the problem, well, you know, because it didn't happen all the time. We were in counseling, and it seemed to be getting better...right? I only added to the onerous weight by beating myself up because I was allowing this abuse to continue.

JUST ONE MORE THING JUST ONE MORE THING JUST ONE MORE THING JUST ONE MORE THING JUST ONE MORE THING JUST ONE MORE THING JUST ONE MORE THING JUST ONE MORE THING JUST ONE MORE THING JUST ONE MORE THING JUST ONE MORE THING JUST ONE MORE THING JUST ONE MORE THING

My good girl continued to
BELIEVE
that if I could do *just one more thing*
all would be better.

That was my home life. In contrast, my work life was very different. AOL was a very positive, affirming place for me. I felt valued and appreciated. I was rewarded for my performance. My creative spirit soared in this entrepreneurial environment. When I was at work, my soul was rejuvenated and the day would rush by. Then, before I knew it, 3:00 p.m. would roll around, and that horrible sinking feeling would start to creep in. I knew in a few hours I would have to go home, where I had to defend my actions, hear criticisms, and feel at risk.

My good girl continued to believe that if I could do just one more thing, the relationship would turn around and all would be better. My good girl kept telling me that he only hit me out of his own hurt and that he really didn't mean it. Yet, my good girl was getting more and more exhausted. I was starting to consider that maybe my life wasn't supposed to be happy after all.

I'm awfully darn serious at the moment. But the truth is that sometimes where our naive, well-intended good girls can lead us is no joke. My experience may be more extreme, but you can see by not being true to ourselves, and by not taking charge or responsibility for our decisions, lives can be ruined. And it happens way too often.

By not being true to ourselves and not taking responsibility for our decisions, lives can be ruined.

Finally I decided I was worth having a better life, no matter what. It happened the evening my husband started to berate me for not taking care of him while he was home sick, even though I'd taken him to the emergency room the evening before, nursed him through the night, went to work after two hours of sleep to give an important presentation, and phoned him throughout the day to see how he was doing. He supposedly gave me his blessing to go off and do what I needed. I thought I was a saint of sorts for doing all this! And he was telling me it wasn't enough!

Hearing his criticisms stirred in me a new level of fury. I started to defend myself, but that only added fuel to his fire. Tension quickly escalated. Then, like a movie flashback, I saw this situation as if I had been here before and knew the ending. This man could not be reasoned with. Right then I decided I was no longer going to let him prey on my good girl. Starting now, access denied.

Then another flash occurred: To deal with the immediate situation, I figured the best thing to do was to become an actress. It didn't matter that I overlooked taking drama in high school. I was motivated! I strategically pricked his rage balloon by profusely confessing how right he was, how I should have acted differently, and how sorry I was. But, I didn't believe a word of it. He did, and that's what mattered – to me and to the Academy (silent applause for me)! I continued to fake it until I'd devised a safe exit plan. Within a few days, we were separated and I was on the road to healing

My internal good girl was hurt, angry, and resentful. My emerging internal Bodacious Woman reminded me of the saying I saw once on a cocktail napkin, "Put your big girl panties on and deal with it!" Dealing with an abusive husband and going through a divorce have been the toughest, most painful things I've done in my life, but also the most empowering. Being a good girl wasn't good enough. To take care of myself, I had to wish the good girl good-bye.

Down With Love?

If you haven't seen the movie *Down with Love* starring Rene Zelleweger and Ewan McGregor, I highly recommend it. It's delightfully cute, funny, and bodacious! As I laughed at the characters' funny clothes and cute remarks, I also noticed their remarks were honest statements about how men and women see the world and what they want in their lives.

The female lead was down with love because love, in her opinion, just weighed her down and led to a constrained life as a suburban housewife. The leading man was a hip, urban swinger with a gadget-filled bachelor pad who had plenty of women to love. The characters seemed at odds, which of course is a great setup for a story.

You'll have to see the movie to see what happens (I'm not going to give it all away). But, I will share this: The overall message of the movie is that women can be empowered. They can be bodacious, and still have love! Strong, Bodacious Women might put some men off, but generally those who are good matches find such women refreshing and attractive.

One reason I think this is true is because Bodacious Women share the load. For many men, carrying the responsibility of working to provide for their families can weigh heavily on them. The happiest couples I know include women who actively shoulder the load (whether they go to work or not). To do that takes energy, determination, and a positive attitude.

Another reason I think men find Bodacious Women attractive is because they are full of life! You don't have to be a Victoria Secret model to be thought of as fun and exciting. But you do have to be aware of who you are and be comfortable expressing your authentic

What's It Worth To You?

Bodacious Woman **Donna Wood**

After I watched several male colleagues rise to levels I felt I deserved, I started to see the value of promoting myself within the company. One BoMo® happened when I applied for a new, highly responsible position. The hiring manager asked me to develop a list of accountabilities for the position. We had a great meeting, and he indicated that he wanted me for the job! Then we talked about compensation. He said he would review my current salary and consider an increase. I countered: "What's this position worth to you?" Based on the responsibility, I knew it was worth more than a 10 or 15% raise. He asked me to suggest a salary, which I promptly supplied. He agreed with my suggestion and I was promoted to a new job that I loved with a 35% increase in salary, plus bonus!

self. I can always spot a Bodacious Woman because her eyes glow and she has a positive energy about her. She's alive! And that's attractive to everyone. Down with love? I don't think so. Up with being bodacious!

The New Good Girl Alternative

It seems to me that most of us continue to be good girls into adulthood because we think there are no alternatives for us. On one end of the spectrum is the good girl, and on the other end, is the b-word, the bitch. There, I said it, as if you didn't know. How can we *not* know? It's the term all women fear far more than good girl!

I don't consider myself a bitch and haven't knowingly been called one, though if I were, it wouldn't bother me, at least not now. You see, there's something about a bitch that I respect: She sticks up for what she wants and makes no bones about it. From that perspective,

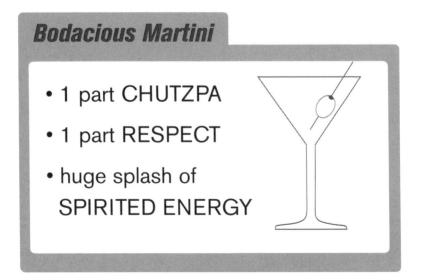

Bodacious Martini

- 1 part CHUTZPA
- 1 part RESPECT
- huge splash of SPIRITED ENERGY

I could wear the baseball cap a friend enthusiastically gave me with the embroidered letters B.I.T.C.H. and the phrase "Babe In Total Control of Herself" scrawled beneath. Oops, maybe I have been called a bitch! I guess I didn't notice – I was having so much fun!

What I'm not so wild about is the bitch's delivery, about how she abuses her power and influence to get what she wants, and about how she seems to be filled with anger most of the time. I just don't want to live that way. At the very least, the negative undertones are an emotional quagmire that would scare small children and a few adults.

So, if being a good girl isn't good enough for taking care of yourself in today's world and being a bitch isn't either, then what's the alternative? Being bodacious, of course! Being bodacious can be thought of as a combination of the bitch chutzpa, good girl respect for others, and a huge splash of positive, spirited energy to boot! Consider it the Bodacious Martini!

Most women I know want to feel empowered. They like to be positive. The key ingredient to creating this powerful elixir is to be authentic. That means looking within and making *you* the reference point to how you see life, and making decisions based on your own internal know-how. It's taking responsibility for determining your view of your world and how you're going to act in it. It's having the courage to be in charge of your life. That's being bodacious!

To further understand the Bodacious Way, I've created the Bodacious Woman Mantra. This mantra breaks down the Bodacious Way into parts that are easy to remember. You can focus on one or two behaviors, or you can absorb larger chunks at any time. It's up to you, which I love, because choice is fundamental to the Bodacious Way.

Exclamation Points

!   You are no longer a *girl*. You're an adult woman!
•   Thinking of yourself as a girl only diminishes your personal power.

!   The main good girl strategy of pleasing others has
•   a big problem – it leaves you open to letting others define who you are, how you feel, and where you're going.

!   Watch out! Where our naive, well-intended good girls
•   can lead us is no joke. By not being true to ourselves, and by not taking charge or responsibility for our decisions, lives can be ruined. And it happens way too often.

!   Being a good girl doesn't work. Being a bitch doesn't
•   either. The alterative is to be bodacious!

3

The Bodacious Woman Mantra

Being a good girl isn't good enough, but being a Bodacious Woman is! So, what does being a Bodacious Woman look like – and how do you do it? Well, first thing, **be relieved that no breast implants are required**. Phew! I know you were wondering. Bodacious Women come in all shapes and sizes. Thank goodness, because variety keeps life interesting. Now that that's off my chest (oh, I just had to say that), let me share with you what I consider the essentials for being a Bodacious Woman. I call it my Bodacious Woman Mantra.

Once you know what makes up the Bodacious Woman Mantra, you'll start noticing these behaviors by Bodacious Women everywhere! In the annals of history, you won't just see Queen Boudicca as a bronze statue in downtown London, you'll see a mini movie in your mind of a strong-willed woman courageously galloping on a horse into battle with her spear raised high and her conviction even higher. In today's news, you won't see a female elected official causing a commotion, you'll see a woman taking a stand for what she believes is right. When you talk with a co-worker who is struggling, you'll see a gutsy woman figuring out the words to say to her manager about her dissatisfaction. In speaking with a neighborhood mother who is hesitant about confronting her teenager about drugs, you'll see a compassionate woman courageously initiating a conversation that may save her child's life. All of these women and many more will inspire you to be your own Bodacious Woman.

The Bodacious Woman Mantra

Look within.
Think strategically.
Act bodaciously.

So, are you ready for the Bodacious Woman Mantra? Are you ready for me to bring it on? Of course you are! Okay, here it is, the saying that women everywhere will be chanting to one another to encourage, empower, and invoke spontaneous celebration. And it's your rallying cry, too. Drum roll please. Ladies and gentlemen, the Bodacious Woman Mantra:

Look within. Think strategically. Act bodaciously. And love every minute of it!

Four simple phrases that can change your life. It's kind of like the timeless fashion principle of less is more. You don't need a big, complex, rocket-science-brain-surgeon concept to change your life, you just need a dress that fits, looks good, and makes you feel like a million bucks inside and out! So, try on the Bodacious Woman Mantra and see how it feels.

Look Within

When you live your life bodaciously, you get more of what you want; loving and respectful relationships, exciting work, and recognition for your contributions. But these are only the *external* manifestations of the Bodacious Way. Bodacious Women know these rewards come easily when you are bodacious *within* first. All the skills, techniques, and savvy in the world won't stick until you improve the quality of your inner messages. **What you say to *yourself* is a major tool in building a fabulous life.**

In her book *Simple Abundance*, Sarah Ban Breathnach wrote:

"Going within opens the eyes of your awareness in gentle ways. You start to treat yourself more kindly. As you become intimate with your authentic self and see glimmers of the woman you truly are inside, you shore up the courage to take the first tentative steps necessary to help her evolve and emerge outwardly."

These words express the process of the authentic path. It starts by looking within and becoming aware of what's happening inside you. What are you saying to yourself about yourself? Do you hear yourself saying things like "you're a good kid," as my mom echoed when I was a child? Or, do you often feel you aren't measuring up and are critical of everything you do? Or, perhaps you don't even know how you feel about yourself, what you think, or what you want. Your good girl might be hanging out without you realizing it. Good girls are so focused on how others feel, they often don't know how *they* feel. It's okay – we can fix that!

Looking within means doing two key things: Trusting your inner voice and protecting your self-esteem.

LOOKING WITHIN
MEANS DOING 2 KEY THINGS

TRUSTING YOUR INNER VOICE PROTECTING YOUR SELF-ESTEEM

Trust Your Inner Voice

Trusting your inner voice means you first have to listen to what's going on inside you. Your Bodacious Inner Voice might be shy at first because you haven't given her much attention. But, don't worry, that won't last long. Get quiet and give her some air time and you'll know exactly what she's thinking. I mean, what you're thinking! And, remember, Bodacious Women know all the good stuff is true. All the not-so-good stuff is just leftover broadcasts from others. These messages have a pesky way of hanging around until we deliberately give them the boot. Pull the plug on those negative internal transmissions!

If you listen carefully, your inner voice will help you determine how you feel about yourself and what you want. The Bodacious Woman trusts her inner voice and moves in that direction. Maybe your inner voice is telling you what you *don't* want, without any real clue yet as to what to reach for instead. That one is guaranteed to worry the people who love you. That happened to me when I decided to take five years of engineering school and not become an engineer. I had chosen engineering because it seemed like a good idea at the time. And my mother wisely pointed out that as one of the few women in the field, I'd be practically guaranteed a high-paying job right out of college.

But during my final year, my inner voice just wouldn't hold her tongue any longer, not that there's anything wrong with engineering as a career, mind you, but whenever I thought about the prospect of doing

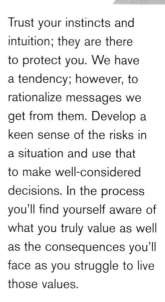

Trust Your Intuition

Trust your instincts and intuition; they are there to protect you. We have a tendency; however, to rationalize messages we get from them. Develop a keen sense of the risks in a situation and use that to make well-considered decisions. In the process you'll find yourself aware of what you truly value as well as the consequences you'll face as you struggle to live those values.

– Bodacious Woman
Deborah Young-Kroeger

that work *for the rest of my life,* I got depressed. It wasn't right for me. It was always an uphill challenge, and whenever I got to the top of the hill, I didn't find the reward exhilarating. I was just grateful not to be sliding back down again. Not a good sign for a future career, wouldn't you say?

There I was, at the beginning of my adult life, having just completed training that prepared me to do something I didn't enjoy. So, without any idea what I would do in its place, I took a very bodacious step. I chose not to take one of the necessary qualifying exams that would position me as a legitimate job candidate. Not only did I slam that door, I locked it and threw away the key!

The only thing my inner voice was telling me was what I *didn't* want to do. I had to let go of the thing I didn't want to do – engineering – before I could grab hold of the next, a lesson I'd keep learning in my career and personal life. I wasn't looking forward to going home with the news, that's for sure. But I felt empowered because I made a choice that I knew in my gut was right for me. It probably didn't help my parents feel any better that my first job would be an $8 an hour entry-level support position with some no-name computer company. But it was most definitely my first step to AOL and a career that far exceeded my dreams and expectations.

Protect Your Self-Esteem

The second key aspect of looking within is to protect yourself from self-esteem busters. Self-esteem is the climate control in your internal house. No matter what is raging outside, when your self-esteem is healthy and functioning, you are safe, dry, and secure within. Unfortunately, **our culture tends to confuse self-esteem with self-absorption, self-centeredness, or just plain old selfishness, and this confusion leads women to be discouraged about taking care of themselves.** It's still seen as somehow charming to be modest to the point of self-deprecation (this old thing?), to be demure to the point of stepping out of our own spotlight created by our hard work in order to make the comfort and happiness of others the hallmark of our own success. Watch out! It's a good girl attack!

It's not charming to siphon off our best energies by playing this foolish, even cowardly, game. It's insincere, unauthentic, and it takes the power from those moments when we are truly humble. Take, for instance, the phrase, *I'm sorry*. How many ways do you use this expression, and frankly, aren't really sorry at all – when you want someone to repeat something, when you need to interrupt a conversation for a legitimate purpose, when you really want to put someone in his place and are hoping that he'll pick up the edge of your biting sarcasm, when your grocery cart is suddenly in the way because another shopper came barreling around the corner? I know it's a common phrase, but Bodacious Women know such language does nothing but dilute our personal power. If you're truly sorry, say so. Otherwise, call it what it is and protect your self-esteem.

Guarding your self-esteem doesn't mean that you care for others any less, it means that you care for yourself more, probably more than you have. To have healthy self-esteem doesn't mean you spend hours gazing in the mirror. It doesn't mean you consider yourself the Queen of All That is Perfect; therefore, everyone should drop to their knees at your feet. It doesn't mean that you cut in line or take the largest piece, but it does mean you serve yourself well.

Having healthy self-esteem means knowing what you value and appreciate. It also means knowing what you don't value. It means choosing friends who share your joie de vivre, and avoiding acquaintances who sap your energy. It means choosing organizations to work for and join that reflect your beliefs and values, and staying away from those that don't. It means celebrating your good news with others. It means loving the body you have, accepting all forms of pleasure as part of your birthright, and joyfully seeking out the people and activities that remind you of how wonderful it is to be alive.

When Strong Wills Start Early

Bodacious Woman **Tiane Mitchell-Gordon**

When your maternal grandmother's pet name is Hellcat and your mother's is Babycakes, you inherit a certain amount of spiciness tempered by sweetness. These women were very strong-willed, who admired and appreciated women like Eleanor Roosevelt and Mary McLeod Bethune. My mother tells me of my first BoMo®. I was three years old, and when my father told me to do something, I stood up, looked him in the eyes and said, "You can't tell me what to do!" My father was shocked at first, and then burst out laughing. His only comment: "Like mother, like daughter."

It means saying yes to those things that bring you joy and satisfaction and no to those things that don't. Good girls have a hard time saying no. Bodacious Women see euphemisms such as "she's not nice" or "she's not a team player" as subtle criticisms of behavior for not falling in line with what someone wants.

Body image and weight are two areas that definitely challenge our self-esteem. There are lots of books, videos, and classes available about how to get in shape and feel good about yourself. I've certainly spent my share on them because I wanted the results they were promising. But like many of us, I had limited success, even with my most disciplined efforts. I still struggled with *wanting* to work hard at trying to get my body to be the ideal image I had in my mind. What I didn't realize is that physical and emotional health is a manifestation of Bodacious Self-Respect! Conversely, the slide out of fitness is a loud signal that there's something wrong that needs addressing.

For instance, before I was married, I used to exercise, eat well, and feel pretty good about my body. But with the strains and challenges to my sense of self-esteem that my marriage created for me, my body, and my happiness reflected my struggles. The week after I left my husband for the last time, I knew I wanted to get back to feeling good about my body and how I looked. Once I reclaimed my self-respect, it was amazing how easy it was to make the time to exercise. I was no longer fighting against myself.

It's not shallow to recognize that when you know you look better, you feel better about yourself as well. We're back to lessons from fashion once again! Ah, the amazing cycle of life!

Look within; that's the first refrain in the Bodacious Woman Mantra. You have to look inside yourself to fully discover who you are and what you want. Listen to and trust your inner voice. Garner your self-esteem and protect it like a jewel. Remember, you're an amazing woman! Deep down you really know that. But don't keep the secret to yourself. We're dying out here wanting to know you in your full regalia! Bring it on, sister!

Think Strategically

Most women, me included, weren't taught to think strategically, not by our parents, not in grade school, not in college, nowhere! Many of us were taught directly or indirectly that someone else – a man (gasp!) – would protect and provide and we wouldn't have to worry our pretty little heads. Sound like leftovers from 1950?! Gimme a break.

Welcome to the twenty-first century (as if you hadn't noticed the date), where the divorce rate is over 50%. Life is a lot more complex and stressful, and we're all trying to figure it out. At the very least, today's woman has to consider who she might marry, if anyone at all, whether she wants a family, what a career might look like, and how she will financially take care of herself into old age. She's got to be fully in charge of her life!

MANY OF US WERE TAUGHT THAT SOMEONE ELSE WOULD PROTECT AND PROVIDE – SOUND LIKE LEFTOVERS FROM 1950?! **GIMME A BREAK.**

The fact is, many women end up being single parents, outliving any men in their lives, and, if they're not careful, they may grow old in poverty (an amazing statistic is that 70% of all widows hardly have enough money to eat). Not thinking strategically about our lives and futures is a train wreck waiting to happen! Don't get me wrong, I'm all for having a good man with whom to share my life. I'm also all for thinking strategically about what I want, how I'm going to get it, and how I'm going to take care of myself. Men worthy of my companionship welcome my Bodacious Woman perspective. (Check out the sidebar *Down With Love?* in Chapter Two for some more commentary on bodacious relationships.)

Know What You Want

When you look within, and trust your inner voice, it's easy to feel affirmed, get excited and want to take action. But wait! Think strategically. **You can't decide *how* to get where you're going until you decide *where* you are going and why. Well, duh.**

But how many times do we race off in the morning, going from one thing to another until we drop? Those days turn into weeks, and weeks turn into months or years, until we're frustrated and confused and say, "Hey, what am I doing?" Or, as the popular psychologist Dr. Phil McGraw would say, "How's that working for ya?"

Good girls follow what they believe to be life's track – without much consideration if it's the track they want to be on. There's the mommy track that goes something like this: Get married, buy a house, have a child, have another child, maybe have a third child, get a bigger house, go on some vacations, launch kids from the nest, retire with husband.

Then there's the career track: Go to college, get an entry-level job, work your way up, change companies, go back to college, become a VP, work like a madwoman, perhaps get promoted to Senior VP or higher, retire with or without husband or significant other.

Bodacious Women don't make all the same choices, but all Bodacious Women make deliberate choices for themselves.

For many women, it's the combo mommy and career track: Go to college, get a starter job, fall in love, get promoted, get married, buy a home, have a child, become a VP, squeeze in an evening MBA, take a few vacations, have another child, don't even think about a third one, buy a bigger house, spring the kids from the nest, remember what your husband looks like, go for your last rung on the career ladder, retire with or without husband. And on and on.

These are just a few of the common tracks women take. A bunch of women are creating a whole new track. It includes ditching their corporate careers to start their own businesses so they can have more control to create a life that's more satisfying for themselves and their family. I call this the "I'm laying down my own d@*& track!"

The point is this: **What track are you on and do you like where it's headed?** Do you know what you want? Have you ever given it much thought? Or, are you simply moving in the direction you believe you were supposed to?

Good girls don't ask themselves such questions and just go along for the ride. Bodacious Women are the conductors of their own trains. They consider the messages they received growing up. They look within to determine how they feel and what's right for them. Bodacious Women don't make all the same choices, but all Bodacious Women make *deliberate* choices for *themselves*.

Strategic thinking isn't limited to the big picture, the long-term stuff of life. There are plenty short-term situations that need this "what do I want?" approach as well. It took me reaching the glass ceiling by not getting promoted to the job I thought I deserved before I realized my lack of strategic thinking.

Here I was the head of corporate training at AOL for 12,000 employees. I'd handled big, company-wide projects successfully, and expanded my focus to include organizational consulting. When the new position of director of organizational development was announced, I thought it had been created just for me. I was doing most of the job already anyway!

But, my boss said I "wasn't strategic enough." No kidding, he actually used those words! Sometimes it takes the obvious for me to get it. What? I thought! He'd never given me that feedback before. Discouraged and disheartened, I left his office, determined to figure out what went wrong. I reflected, I spoke with a few trusted colleagues, and you know what? I didn't agree with his conclusion! I figured there was no way I could have been effective in these big projects if I didn't think of the big picture of how the company worked and how to get people involved.

But, here's what I didn't do – where he was right. I didn't consider *all* the ways I needed to communicate what I was doing and how it tied in to large company goals. I needed to promote my efforts and results. I needed to embrace office politics and leverage them in my favor. Now, *that* would have been strategic! In retrospect, what I wanted was to perform well *and* get recognized for it. I figured out how to do the first part, but I never got clear about the recognition part, and therefore, hardly did it. If I had been more strategic, it's very possible I would have avoided the glass ceiling altogether. Instead, I learned an extremely valuable lesson.

Which brings me to another key behavior of thinking strategically: Focus on what's going right.

Focus on What's Going Right

When you know what you want and you start trying to make it happen, things won't always go as planned. Count on it. **Life is messy, and we're living in an age when it's getting messier everyday. You can shrink into a hole if you want to, though that**

never seemed like a smart beauty move to me, unless, of course, you add some water for a mud bath. I was actually going to do a mud bath one time until I realized I was going to be sharing the space with a few creepy, crawly bugs. I decided this was not my definition of a love bug. What we women won't do to look gorgeous!

But mud and mess aren't necessarily bad. There's a lot of opportunity in any situation. Seriously, I mean it! You've just got to be willing to see it. I like to think of it as response-ability. As a Bodacious Woman, I know I have the ability to respond to situations. Circumstances don't dictate my reactions unless I *let* them.

Sure you're mad and hurt, there's no denying it. Let it out – to a friend, spouse, or someone you trust. Once released, decide if you will continue to be in that place or if you're going to see what's there for you to learn from and grow. Good girls tend to be in shock when life throws them a curve ball and things don't go as expected. Bodacious Women know that stuff happens, even with the best of intentions. They see things for what they are, accept their feelings, and strategically focus on what's going right and what they can gain.

There's a ton of leverage in focusing on what's going right. Often when I speak to groups of women about what it means to be bodacious, I ask them to fill out a short quiz to determine just how bodacious they already are. Some women don't see themselves as bodacious until it's in black and white.

They assess their bodaciousness by rating themselves on a scale of 1 to 5; 5 means they behave this way most of the time and 1 means not so much. When I ask who circled a 4 or 5 on any one of the statements, proud hands shoot up all over the room. Women are energized by acknowledging their own bodaciousness. Then I ask

on a
scale of

1 *to* **5**

How
bodacious
*Are **You?***

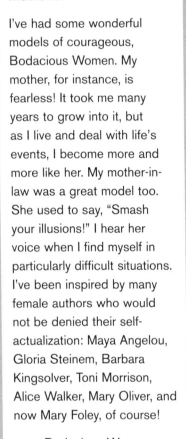

Smash Your Illusions!

I've had some wonderful models of courageous, Bodacious Women. My mother, for instance, is fearless! It took me many years to grow into it, but as I live and deal with life's events, I become more and more like her. My mother-in-law was a great model too. She used to say, "Smash your illusions!" I hear her voice when I find myself in particularly difficult situations. I've been inspired by many female authors who would not be denied their self-actualization: Maya Angelou, Gloria Steinem, Barbara Kingsolver, Toni Morrison, Alice Walker, Mary Oliver, and now Mary Foley, of course!

– Bodacious Woman
Deborah Young-Kroeger

them if they rated themselves a 1 or 2 for any of the items. Many of the same hands go up, though this time sheepishly. They don't feel completely bodacious...yet. Okay, so what? Tell me something I don't know. Neither am I. It's a continuous process and adventure.

To really grow, the best strategy is to first recognize how bodacious you're already are. This approach fills you up and gives you the spunk to try some new behaviors and make progress in other areas. Wallowing in how you're not very bodacious gets you nowhere.

Want to take my fun "How Bodacious Are You?" quiz for yourself? You can! Just go online to my website www.GoBodacious.com. You'll see it there on the home page. It takes about two minutes and at the end I offer you some practical ways to fully become the Bodacious Woman you want to be.

One of my favorite sayings comes from author Richard Bach, in his book *Illusions*. At one point in the story, the main character says to the other lead, "Argue for your limitations and they're yours." If you believe you really can't do something or the situation really does stink so much that it boxes you in, then you know what, you're right!

Focusing on what's going right doesn't mean being in denial about what needs fixing. But putting most of your attention and energy in the direction of those things that are working and helping you feel good about yourself gives you the necessary self-esteem and staying power for dealing with difficult situations and creating change in your life.

Act Bodaciously

Are you lovin' the Bodacious Woman Mantra so far? Looking within, trusting your inner voice, and protecting

Bodacious By Choice

I became bodacious by choice, when I figured out I could be. I grew up shy, but it was hard to avoid the limelight when I took the path of an engineering degree and ended up one of five women in a 500-man engineering department. And, again later when I got my law degree and ended up as the second woman partner at a 75-attorney firm. Over time, I realized that I could either avoid the limelight and continue to think I was only play-acting at being an engineer and an attorney, or I could find my voice, value my own worth, and be what I said I was —a competent engineer and an excellent attorney. So after trying it out, speaking my mind, and exercising the power I had, I figured out I could and would be bodacious.

– Bodacious Woman
   Nancy Regelin

your self-esteem made you feel pretty good about yourself I'll bet. Taking the time to think strategically by knowing what you want and by focusing on what's going right is pretty cool, too. There's no doubt in my mind that bodaciousness starts on the inside. But at some point, you need to go public! It's time to act bodaciously for all the world to see. Don't worry, they're gonna love you. And, if not, oh well, how can your old good girl ways ever be *this* satisfying?

Bodacious Women know what their dreams are, and they lay out an effective path to make them come true. Have you noticed how many people are more committed to the dream itself, rather than accomplishing that dream? These are the people who are always talking about some day, or about their frustrations or their anger or their irritation at repeatedly falling short of the mark. These are the people who are in love with the wish, rather than being fully committed to making the wish happen.

For Bodacious Women, dreams aren't just wispy castles in the air. They are the end point to strategic planning. For Bodacious Women, goals are never beyond their reach. But, they're well aware of the fact that they may have to stretch to grab a solid hold on their objectives. Maybe they have to learn a new skill or new language. Maybe they need to break the habits of certain self-definitions: They've been overweight all their lives, they can't save a penny, they're always negative or impatient, or they don't have a head for math or computers. Bodacious Women know there are steps from here to there, and that those steps can be discovered.

Say What You Want

When you're ready to bring your bodaciousness more to the forefront, there's going to be one good girl way that won't want to let go. It's the tendency to hold back from coming right out and

Dreams aren't just wispy castles in the air.

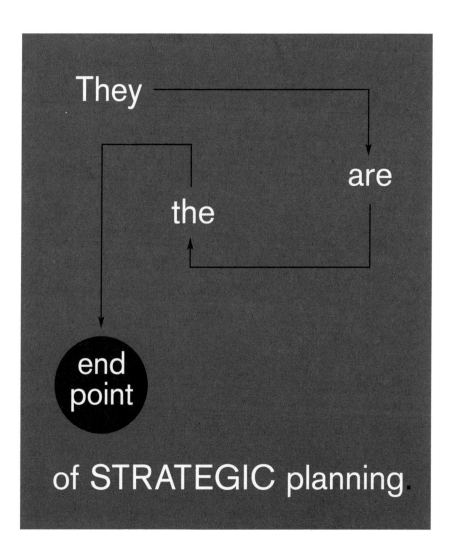

They ⟶ are

the

end point

of STRATEGIC planning.

clearly saying what you want. Good girls hope that people kinda sorta understand what they want by inference. "Going to that restaurant would be nice. This other one is nice, too, don't you think?" "It would help me a lot if you could get me those numbers as soon as possible." Oh, come on! You *know* which restaurant you prefer. You *know* when you need those numbers in order to meet your deadline. So say so!

Maybe you're thinking that it's not nice to be so direct. It feels a bit harsh. Think again, sister! On the contrary, it's not nice to so muffle your communication that others don't know what you want, that you don't say what you need, and that the both of you are left frustrated and full of blame. Most people are willing to help you out and give you what you want (especially if it's easy and within reason). Likely you do things for others as well, just because it feels good. Bodacious Women know you're not being harsh by coming out and clearly saying what you want; you're doing everyone involved a favor.

Here's a tip to make "I want this" seem a bit softer if you're still a bit hesitant. Use two magical words: I need. When someone legitimately needs something, it's hard to ignore them or turn them down. Okay, so we're not talking, "I need this fabulous mink coat to stay warm. It sometimes drops to 40 degrees, you know." I'm talking, "I need you to be standing outside by the school gym doors at 4:30 p.m. so we can get ahead of the traffic." Or, "I appreciate your work in this project. I need that software fix to be completed by Friday so we can go on to the next step by Monday. Can you do that?"

And guess what? When you get up the guts to act bodaciously and clearly say what you want, you might get a big fat *no* for all your efforts. Why, then, go to all the trouble? Why not just let things go along as before and see what happens? I'll tell you why! Because

MY THEORY:
I get "NO" anyway by not asking.

NOT ASKING	ASKING
NOT ASKING	ASKING
NOT ASKING	ASKING
NOT ASKING	ASKING
NOT ASKING	ASKING
NOT ASKING	ASKING
NOT ASKING	ASKING
NOT ASKING	ASKING
NOT ASKING	ASKING
+ NOT ASKING	+ ASKING

NO

MAYBE
YES!

shrinking back and being a good girl does nothing for your self-esteem and nothing for your own empowerment.

My theory is this: I was getting *no* anyway by not asking.

The only way to get a firm yes to what I want is to clearly put it out there. Sometimes I get a *No, but...*, which usually means I can get some of what I want or an alternative that works just as well. Even if I get a flat-out *no*, I figure I'm not losing, because I'm keeping my bodacious muscle in shape. I am a force to be reckoned with. Just look at all the BoMos® and advice from Bodacious Women throughout this book. These triumphs and insights clearly reflect women who know what they want and know how to go for it!

Don't Over Explain, Don't Over Complain

Here's another tip for saying what you want: Don't over explain; don't over complain. This wisdom I picked up from the late, great Katharine Hepburn. Talk about a Bodacious Woman! (See my sidebar in Chapter One.) Hepburn knew it would be tough to be a successful female actress in the male-dominated acting world of the 1930s. She didn't let that dissuade her. She worked hard *and* smart.

One of her smart, Bodacious Ways was not to express her opinions as if she were giving testimony to a jury. How many good girls do you know who do that? I've seen time and again in the workplace a competent, intelligent woman explain to the nth degree why she made a decision, including all the background events of who said what and who did what and then what happened, and then...! I cringe as I watch her stature and power seep out of the room. It's just not necessary! In fact, it goes against her entire effort to be thought of as credible and to be taken seriously. *It's so much more powerful to say what you want or what you did, add a few words, and then shut up.* If others have questions, they'll ask! And you can decide if and how much to answer.

The same principle applies when it comes to complaining. We all know life isn't always a good time and there's much to gripe about if we want to. But, big-time complainers are downright irritating. When it's important enough, Bodacious Women do something about it. They take a stand. They go to the person, express how they feel, say their peace, and do their part to cause things to change. Going on and on won't help. In fact, it usually hurts your stance.

A very unbodacious behavior when you take a stand is to keep expounding on how awful the event was, how you felt, how it affected others, what that means for your future, how you can't imagine anyone being so mean...until you've beaten the other person up so much they either come back with a vengeance or relinquish themselves to your battering and resent you for it.

The Bodacious Way means honoring yourself as well as honoring others. Explaining or complaining to some extent honors yourself. Overdoing it doesn't honor anyone and zaps your bodacious power. Don't over explain, don't over complain, and learn to take a stand (Groove on this further by checking out my sidebar, *6 Steps for Taking a Stand.*).

6 Steps for Taking a Stand

1. **Trust your inner voice that says something's not right.**

   If something feels wrong to you about a situation or person at work, it probably is. We may not know exactly why just yet, but the first step to effectively managing conflict is to believe that there's a problem. Good girls tend to deny or minimize a problem. Bodacious Women don't look away or pretend. They accept that a problem exists.

2. See the situation for what it is.

After you've accepted that a problem exists, back off from your frustration for the moment and use your head to paint as complete a picture as possible. Who are all the players or people involved? What are the facts of the situation (for example, he did this, then she said that, then I said...)? What underlying dynamics do you also see going on? Try to be as objective as possible at this point. It's easy to get emotionally swept up and thrown off as you think through this. Resist that as much as possible.

3. Decide what you want.

Here's where you first need to take a stand with yourself. In almost all the conflicts we have, there is usually some aspect that attacks our sense of self-worth or self-esteem. Standing up for yourself first means you internally reject negative, critical messages from others as true, and believe that you are a person worth being treated with respect.

Now that you're clear about being treated with respect, what do *you* want to be different in this situation? Is there a specific behavior you want the other person to demonstrate? Is there a specific decision or result you want in your favor? Be as specific as possible, because when you are, you're more likely to get it.

4. Decide how you're going to interact with this person.

Determine what you're going to say and how you're going to say it. If you're saying something in person, write it out and say it out loud. Start with a statement of your main point, pause, and then add backup information of what you mean and why you feel the way you do. No need to over explain. Practice in front of mirror, then on a trusted friend who can give you feedback. Get used to the wording so that it flows without having to look down at your paper. If you're writing an e-mail or letter, write it once, then put it aside and read it again later. Is it clear? Is it too long? Would the person know how you want them to respond? Again, ask a friend to put their eyes on it and get feedback.

5. Do it!

You just gotta get started and do it! I know that taking a stand in person is a tough thing to do; yet often it's the most effective way to get your needs met. I also know we have to face our fears head on. One thing that helps me is to focus on the fact that I can't fail. Why? Because the fact is, I didn't shrink from the uncomfortable situation, I demonstrated my self-respect, and I'm doing something about it.

6. Expect some pushback and then respond.

Once you've determined what you're going to say and how you're going to say it, anticipate the response. If you're addressing one person, come up with at least two ways he or she may respond. How will you reply? If it's a small group, consider at least one response for each person.

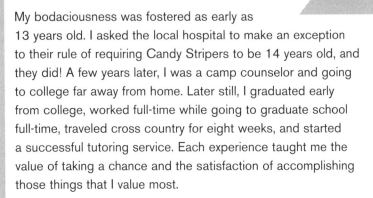

The Value of Taking a Chance

My bodaciousness was fostered as early as 13 years old. I asked the local hospital to make an exception to their rule of requiring Candy Stripers to be 14 years old, and they did! A few years later, I was a camp counselor and going to college far away from home. Later still, I graduated early from college, worked full-time while going to graduate school full-time, traveled cross country for eight weeks, and started a successful tutoring service. Each experience taught me the value of taking a chance and the satisfaction of accomplishing those things that I value most.

– Bodacious Woman Leslie Fagert

Take a Risk

Bodacious Women know that to get anywhere in life takes risk. They also know that the biggest risk is not taking one at all.

Ongoing growth and development requires you to step into new territory and try new behaviors. You've got to take risks! I'm not talking reckless risks. I'm suggesting that you ease into a gutsy life by trial runs; start with smaller challenges, then work outward from there.

For example, let's say next time you eat out, you order something you've never eaten before. **How do you know if you don't like sushi if you've never tried it? Honestly, I thought raw fish was kind of creepy and gross until I gave it a shot.** Nowadays I don't even do the rice part. I go straight for the fish – or eel or octopus – by itself with some open-my-sinuses-right-up green wasabi sauce. From a woman who still thinks most cooked fish tastes too fishy, this is an amazing thing. I never would've known I liked the stuff unless I took a risk and gave it a try.

Now let's suppose – just suppose – that I didn't like sushi after all. Sitting in front of me is a whole plate of circles of rice and fish, and after the first taste I just want to throw up. What's a girl to do? Well, a good girl would pick at it, maybe force a few more bites down, and offer to share it with others. Goodness knows she couldn't admit she hates the stuff and is dreaming about raiding the Krispy Kreme doughnuts when she gets home.

Rewind the tape and insert a Bodacious Woman. She finds she doesn't like sushi, either. But, thinking strategically, she only ordered an appetizer portion just in case things didn't work out. If she liked it, she knew she could order more. Instead of feeling guilty that she took a risk, she quickly admits the results of her experiment: Sushi sucks (at least according to her taste buds). She sends it back and orders something else. Maybe she spends an extra seven bucks. Big whoop. That's a small price to pay for exercising her bodaciousness.

Taking a risk to order a new food is one thing. It's fun and good practice. Taking a risk regarding something of greater consequence really challenges your tolerance of *yikes*! Let's say you've been asked to speak in front of the adult group where you worship, or you need to talk to the childcare director about why your child is suddenly obstinate, or you want to ask your

---

Falure is not trying. Failure is not trynig. Failure is not tr ying. Failure is notrying. Failure iss not trying. (Failure is not trying.)

manager to pay for you to speak at an industry conference, or you want to leave your job to pursue your dream of starting your own business. Now you're getting uncomfortable!

If you try to do any of these things, you could experience the four-letter word you want to avoid more than cellulite: Fail. Fail (gasp)! Let's put it out there, you don't want to fail, and if you take a risk in doing any of these things or more, that might just happen. **Well, *of course*, you might fail. Why did you think you were so uptight in the first place?**

May I suggest you're thinking about failure the wrong way, the unproductive way. Think about it this way: Failure is *not trying*. Read that again. Failure is not trying. Giving something a shot that doesn't work out as planned doesn't mean you're a failure, it means you're a Bodacious Woman demonstrating her guts and courage.

Maybe you want to take a risk but you're so paralyzed you can't move forward. You can't make a decision. Being in this place is no party! At one point in my AOL career, I was debating whether or not to ask my manager for what I wanted: To go part-time. I had recently been accepted to grad school and I quickly determined that continuing to do 60-hour weeks at AOL along with grad school while finalizing my divorce was too much. I didn't want to leave AOL altogether, but part-time was an oxymoron at that place! And anyways, we didn't have a part-time position in my group. Once I voiced my request they (the big powers that be) would know I was pulling back and they could decide I should leave like *now*. I was stuck and afraid. What to do? What to do? What to do?

I was stuck in this quandary. Then a way to get unstuck came to me. You can use it, too, for those sticky, stucky moments. Check out my sidebar below, *How to Get "Unstuck" and Make a Decision.*

By the way, to finish my story about wanting to ask for part-time at AOL, I *did* ask, and my manager *did* give it to me! I was thrilled until I figured out that part-time still meant almost 40-hour work-weeks. After a few months, I opted for zero-time and left AOL.

How to Get "Unstuck" and Make a Decision

1. **Imagine the worst-case scenario of the decision you're trying to make or the risk you want to take.**

    Sit down, tell it to a friend or someone you trust, and paint the complete picture with all the events, people, and especially your feelings. From your cozy chair, experience as much as possible what the worst case would feel like.

2. **Ask yourself what you would do if this worse case happened.**

    What would you do? What would you say? To whom? How might they react? How would you react? If you can answer these kind of questions with some degree of confidence, then you can handle it. It may not be fun, it may not be pretty, but you can handle it. Likely, you've handled something at least as intense before. Remember?

3. **Ask yourself the likelihood of the worse case happening.**

    Most of the time, we paint the most horrible picture, and then it doesn't materialize. It's a great monument to our imagination. Perhaps more of us should write movie

screen plays. So, something between Terrific! and Ugh!
is probably reality. Hey, good news! You've already
determined you can handle that, too. Piece of cake.
Make a decision and go for it!

Love Every Minute of It

Are we having fun yet? Well, of course we are! Every day in every way, you're becoming more bodacious! The Bodacious Woman Mantra starts with looking within because it's up to each of us to understand who we are and to believe our worth in order to create the life we want. To create that life, we need to think strategically about where we're going and why, and then act bodaciously to get there.

If you've mustered the courage to be a Bodacious Woman, I'm sure you've had several discussions with your internal good girl that go something like this: Now listen to me. You were okay to get started in this life, but things are more demanding and more complex than I thought. And, there's too much out there for me to miss if I don't change some of my ways. I can't be a good girl or any *girl* for that matter. I'm a *woman* now, and a bodacious one at that! You can join in and become bodacious with me. Otherwise, don't bug me anymore.

As you continue to live the Bodacious Woman Mantra, I've got one last piece of advice: Love every minute of it! Learn to love the ups and the downs. Laugh and play along the way and life will never get boring. Neither will you!

Thrive on Shift and Change

We all go through tough times when it seems all we can do it simply hang out. But Bodacious Women want to become experts at thriving, not just surviving. Say for instance, you've fallen overboard in a stormy

SHIFT & CHANGE

shift & ***CHANGE***

SHIFT & CHANGE

SHIFT & CHANGE

SHIFT & CHANGE

SHIFT & **CHANGE**

SHIFT & CHANGE

SHIFT & *Change*

...our lives are filled with *shift* and *change*!

sea. The only thing you can see is a buoy within your reach. Naturally, you grab on to it. The question is, will you ever be willing to let go? Too many people become experts of the buoy; they are experts in the art of survival. They know everything about its paint, the texture of its surface, the way it smells, the sound of its bell, and when its beacon flashes. But that won't get them anywhere. Holding on tightly may help you personally and professionally – for a while. It's easy to forget it's only a temporary solution. Eventually, you've got to let go, start swimming, and make progress again.

It's bodacious to let go of the buoy and figure out how to thrive. Hanging on isn't good enough when you're bodacious; neutral doesn't cut it, neither does maintenance. Even though these positions may seem beneficial, they're really keeping you oriented toward fear and prevention of worst-case scenarios. Like I said, chances are the worst case won't happen. And, if it does, you can manage it. Yes, you *can*!

If there's nothing else carved on my tombstone, I hope it says: "Here lies a Bodacious Woman who knew how to thrive on shift and change." Shift and change, shift and change, our lives are filled with shift and change! I learned this important lesson at AOL. Nothing remained the same for me during my 10-year stint: I survived over six layoffs. I moved 10 times. I had 12 different workspaces. I got married and divorced. I was promoted four times. I owned three different cars. The only thing that remained constant was my black vinyl portfolio with a fake reptile pattern that I purchased for my first interview with the company at age 23. Eventually that changed, too. I lost it a year ago at a speaking engagement. Bummer! I guess that means it's time for an upgrade!

I believe the 1990s revealed just a taste of the rate of changing times the world can expect. Hold onto your hats, Bodacious Women, the ride has just begun! We might as well enjoy it (because if nothing else, the alternative really stinks). Personally, I don't think the sky is falling, but life is definitely changing dramatically and that can increase our feelings of insecurity and chaos. It certainly has for me!

We all want security. **My life experience has forced me to come to a conclusion that I resisted in one form or another for a long time: Security is an illusion.** We've all heard that life doesn't come with guarantees, but do we really want to believe that?

Money won't bring security. Sure, it provides some comforts and advantages, but some of the richest people in the world are unhappy and insecure about their future. Relationships don't guarantee security, either. One word proves that: Divorce. A fabulous house may indeed be fabulous, but many people's homes have been damaged or destroyed by hurricanes, tornadoes, and all sorts of disasters. Wonderful kids offer tremendous satisfaction, but they don't always act so wonderfully. All good things that you want in your life are just that – good – but they can't guarantee you will feel good

Don't Get Caught Up in the Day's Trauma

Always remember to be true to your values. Take time to nurture your soul. Keep a sense of humor. Be present in the moment, but plan for the future. Try not to get caught up in the "trauma" of the day by remembering the "big picture". Most importantly, remember, you define your success!

– Bodacious Woman
  Leslie Fagert

about yourself, make you happy, or relieve you of problems. Even an insurance policy doesn't cover everything. Nothing is entirely certain or secure.

Ultimately, security comes from within. Most of the things or people we hope will offer security are outside of ourselves. What's *out there* can't bring us true security; it's what's *in here* that we have to rely on in the big scheme of things. External circumstances may shake us up and cause temporary problems and pain. The Bodacious Woman knows she has the resources inside herself to handle situations and to thrive on shift and change. (Many faiths point to a higher being that gives us inner strength.) No matter what happens, you have yourself, and given what you've handled in the past, that's enough.

The good news is that there's wisdom in uncertainty. Sounds like another oxymoron, doesn't it? You might be thinking, Wisdom in uncertainty? You've got to be kidding! Hold on and I'll explain.

By being uncertain, we stay open to all the possible solutions or ideas regarding any issue. But many women I know are intense planners. Whether they're moms managing a household with children or whether they're company managers in charge of dozens of employees, they have to handle countless details in order to keep things going.

Personally, I'm a big J on the Myers-Briggs assessment. If you have no idea what I'm referring to, just think planner to the max. So I'm all for creating a plan to achieve what I want; it's one of the big reasons I was promoted at AOL. However, life experience has taught me that to thrive on shift and change means I need to approach achieving goals with a more flexible approach. I still need to be very clear about my goals and desires and be very in touch with myself. What I don't need to do is get locked into the path to get there. I can still plan, but also be open to change. By not being overly attached to the details of my plans, I'm open to opportunities to learn, grow, or do things differently, and perhaps better.

Scan the car radio dial until you find a song you like and belt it out at the top of your lungs. Who cares if you look like a *Karaoke on wheels*?

In the small Virginia town where I grew up, the carnival came once a year, with a big circus wheel, haunted house, and other wild delights. When my parents took my sister and me, I was always overwhelmed by the number of rides and games. This circus image comes to mind when I think about thriving on shift and change. I imagine a colorful scene with lots going on. I'm alert to all that's happening around me and I pay attention to the rides and booths to which I'm most attracted. I choose one ride and booth after another, soaking in the experience until the carnival is over. If a thunderstorm suddenly blows in, I immediately figure out where to find shelter. When the rain stops, I decide what to do next (or my parents decide it's time to leave! I am still a young child, after all).

This is a picture of how to thrive on shift and change. Acknowledge the chaos and swirl. Survey the landscape and choose what you'd like to experience. Stay alert to opportunities and enjoy them while you can. And, handle change as it happens. "This too, shall pass" was one of my grandmother Spunky Ethel's sayings. The tough stuff passes, but so does the good stuff, too. Life can be like a carnival if you decide up front to love every minute of it!

Attitude is Everything

I am constantly striving to be more playful and carefree. Attitude is everything, so pick a good one!

– Bodacious Woman
Ruth Cope

Be Playful and Curious

I know you're serious about trying to be a Bodacious Woman. But I caution you. All this thriving on shift and change can wear down even the most Bodacious Woman. To stay energized and engaged, **you've got to be serious about not being so serious!** Don't miss the fun along the way. Be playful! Or, perhaps that's play-Full. Take it from a woman who has deliberately gone from a Type A personality to an A-/B+, laugh as much as possible and find the humor that's begging to be discovered.

There are so many opportunities to be playful every day: Leave a voice mail that sounds like a news report rather than the standard message, spontaneously grab a cup of coffee or tea with a friend or co-worker and share the most comical thing that has happened to you so far that day (this is like a double-espresso. You get one shot from the caffeine and other one from the laughter), scan the car radio dial until you find a song you like and belt it out at the top of your lungs. Who cares if you look like a Karaoke on wheels? Okay, maybe the good girl, but you've already decided not to listen to her any longer. When you allow yourself to play, the demands of your fast, full life temporarily melt away.

Never Stop Learning

Choose to be bodacious. Keep trying it on. Get comfortable with it. Enjoy the company of other Bodacious Women; their spirits are contagious. Be a role model; support other women in their growth. Never stop learning.

– Bodacious Woman Nancy Regelin

Another way Bodacious Women continue to stay vital is by being curious about new things to learn, do, and explore. The Bodacious Woman seeks to expand her understanding of the world, the people, places, cultures, philosophies, and occupations. She finds lifelong learning exciting. There is always something new to discover for the Bodacious Woman. She is rarely bored. She recognizes that learning opportunities are everywhere – not just in the classroom. They happen at dinner, online, at the playground, on television, while reading a book, or when chatting with friends.

There's a big world out there of neat, interesting activities and things to learn. A Bodacious Woman knows she doesn't have to believe everything she hears or adopt everything into her value system. Seeking to understand other people's perspectives helps keep life interesting, but it doesn't confuse her own sense of what's best for her personally. This is especially important in a diverse world.

Playing music is one sure way that helps me let go of daily demands and stresses. Something just starts to happen inside me when singers like Bonnie Raitt playfully deliver such lines as, "Let's run naked through these city streets. We're all captives of captivity...Let's get back to the fundamental things." I can't help myself; I *must* sing along! Then my fingers start snapping and my hips start swaying. I'm sorry, was I just having a stress-filled moment? Oh, well, I'll get back to that later. This music is calling my name!

In the spirit of being playful and keeping life interesting, I've started a new family holiday tradition. It's easy to do when it's your home they come to for the big dinner! Okay, so two years running may not constitute a tradition yet, but needless to say, don't expect the usual turkey and mashed potatoes if you come to my place for Christmas (or insert your alternate traditional holiday here). Instead, expect to ask, "What country are we doing this year?"

The first year, we had an Italian theme. Why? Because I love everything about the place – the food, the wine, the design, the Italian love for life – and being that it was my home, I got to make the rules! I chose the Italian menu and assigned everyone to bring something. It was a quite a *ciao* and *bella* affair! The second year was even more creative. With the help of my sister and my brother's fiancé, we decided upon Cuba. During the tropical Cuban mixed drinks, empanadas, and some weird but tasty yam and black bean soup, we decided to starting opening gifts.

This was my Dad's idea; he's such a smart man! As a father of three daughters and a husband of one Bodacious Woman, he knew that combining the activities of drinking, eating, and opening presents would make us very happy and nourish us with at least three important life-sustaining activities. (Some of the others are not covered in this book, but I bet you could gander a guess!)

The gift opening process was almost a ritual in and of itself. Only one person at a time would unwrap one present while we all watched

in anticipation as if we were going home with whatever it was. And the funnier, the better was our motto! It was either my first or second time to open a gift – I'm not sure which because it was after a few of those darn tasty tropical drinks – that I opened what would transform this already delightful family gathering into party territory never before experienced.

It was a double CD set of top disco hits from my mother (need I say more about her). Not just one CD of shake your groove thing music, but two! Once I read the playlist, which included "YMCA" and "I Will Survive," the seed was planted. Our toes started tapping. First they tapped over to the kitchen to bring the main course of Cuban marinated pork and veggies to the table. Thoroughly fueled up, my sister announced, "Okay, put on the music. It's time for us Cuban wannabees to disco!" I could tell in her voice she was not fooling around.

Then it happened. The irrepressible disco beat started, and within sixty seconds, we were all up from the table wildly dancing and shouting "Y - M - C -A!" while our arms obediently gestured each letter. To this day, I can honestly say I've never had so much fun as an adult at Christmas. And that was before the cigars! As fun as that was, there's always an opportunity to outdo ourselves next year. And goodness knows we'll try. Or, as another Bonnie Raitt song goes, "Let's give 'em something to talk about!"

To love every minute of being a Bodacious Woman means you're always willing to learn and discover new parts of yourself. For example, other cultures can be the stimulus. Take a Spanish class or join a new Scottish country-dancing troupe. A benny of being curious and continuing to learn and grow is that you become every more interesting to others, including your significant others or loved ones. More than anything, life remains interesting to you and you're an active participant.

So, There You Have It!

So, there you have it, the Bodacious Woman Mantra. Let's practice so you can recall these four life-changing phrases whenever you need them. Repeat after me: Look within. Think strategically. Act bodaciously. Love every minute of it!

In classic cheerleader style, let me hear you again: (By the way, being a cheerleader has really progressed since my high school days from a Barbie-like style and cuteness to gymnast athleticism.)

Look where? *Inside!*

Think what? *Strategically!*

Act how? *Bodaciously!*

Love when? *Every minute of it!*

Congratulations, you've got it! Oh, oh, oh, I'm so proud of you! You've considered what it takes to be a Bodacious Woman. You've decided to face your internal good girl. You've started trying new behaviors. And you're feeling more authentic, more powerful, and more alive because of it. Don't let it stop there! Keep growing in your bodaciousness and remember to do what we all need to – bring others along!

The Bodacious Woman Mantra

Look Within

- Trust your inner voice
- Protect your self-esteem

Think Strategically

- Know what you want
- Focus on what's going right

Act Bodaciously

- Say what you want
- Don't over explain, don't over complain
- Take a risk

Love Every Minute of It!

- Thrive on shift and change
- Be playful and curious

Exclamation Points!

! Look within. Trust your inner voice and protect your
   self-esteem. Remember, you're an amazing woman!
   Take my fun "How Bodacious Are You?" quiz online at
   www.GoBodacious.com to find out just how amazing
   you already are.

! Think strategically. Know what you want and focus
   on what's going right. Proactively decide what life
   track you want to be on and spend most of your
   attention on what's working.

! Act bodaciously. Say what you want, don't over
   complain or over explain, and take risks. Go public
   with your Bodacious Woman self! It's time for all the
   world to see.

! Love every minute of it. Thrive on shift and change,
   and be playful and curious. Learn to love the ups and
   the downs. Laugh and play along the way and life will
   never get boring.

4

Bodacious Is Contagious

"It ain't the age, it's the attitude!" That's what it says underneath one of my favorite desk photos of a baby wearing sunglasses, playfully sitting in a box. The older I get, the more I understand and appreciate what this phrase means. On account of this bodacious stuff entering my life, I cooked up my own flavor of this pearl of wisdom. Here it is: It ain't the bod, it's the bodaciousness! Can you relate? The older I get and the more my bod changes in ways I wish it wouldn't, the more I *really* understand and *really* appreciate what it means to have a bodacious attitude!

Being a Bodacious Woman starts on the inside. By trusting your inner voice, you will start to feel more confident and at peace with yourself. Does it mean that you never panic? Never get anxious? Never feel confused? Never feel you've received the short end of the proverbial stick now and then? No. But it does mean you'll have a better way to cope with life's challenges. When you prevail, your successes will pave the way to thrive, rather than merely survive.

Breaking Through to Bodaciousness

Bodaciousness doesn't just happen overnight. It's a process. Make every challenge you face an opportunity to choose the Bodacious Way. With each new risk, your new bodacious muscle is exercised. Soon you'll find yourself saying yes or no when you *really* want to, and relishing the confidence that your bodaciousness is holding tight. As you continue to apply the Bodacious Woman Mantra, you'll understand how the changes, even the frightening ones, that unfold in your life can usher you into improved circumstances – a better job, for instance, a more desirable home, better relationships, a better selection of far more attractive choices. The sky's the limit! Choose to be a Bodacious Woman and watch your good karma unfold. You're breaking through to bodaciousness!

Choose to be a
Bodacious Woman
and watch your good karma unfold.

Bodaciousness is high-performance living! As much as bodaciousness improves your internal climate, it also shows up very quickly on the outside as well. As you become more relaxed, confident, and certain of what you're trying to achieve through your changed behavior, and most importantly, your perceptions about yourself (good girl no more!), those changes will manifest themselves in huge strides in your life as a whole. They'll show up in small and large ways. BoMos® will be everywhere!

Even better, since you'll be thinking more strategically and acting more bodaciously, you'll also be equipped to notice those changes.

I Surprised Myself

Bodacious Woman **Tracy Kinard**

I was a Medical Social Worker for 11 years. I finally came to the conclusion that I was going to be in the same job with no promotion for the rest of my life if I didn't do something about it. I decided to completely change course and become a Financial Planner. I studied like crazy and took some very hard exams, then started my practice. Wow! I didn't know I had it in me. However, that is not the end of the story. I have now decided to stay home with my 3-year-old son and start my own business. I have completely surprised myself!

Congratulate yourself! When you have your objectives clearly defined, expressed, and supported, you'll be better prepared to observe when you've achieved your goals. Then you'll confidently be able to identify what works for you, and build on your successes again and again. You'll start whispering, "Zoom! Zoom!" like they do in those Mazda car commercials!

This is a huge improvement over the unbodacious, good girl way, which is to focus on what's wrong and then not give yourself a moment's peace until all your problems have been solved. Which, of course, is never.

In your unbodacious moments, you can get caught up in internal critical questions such as: Do I deserve to put my task at hand down and enjoy an activity? Do I deserve to be physically fit and look great in clothes? Do I deserve to take that seat at the conference table? Do I deserve to have a happy marriage? Do I deserve to be a great mom to my kids?

The unbodacious answer is No, of course not! How could I possibly think I deserve any of these things? Do you feel there's always something you first need to improve, to work on, to create, to serve, or to fix <u>before</u> you can really enjoy life and feel proud of who you've become?

Sheesh, what a load! I like the bodacious answer better:

Bring it on!

Being bodacious is contagious, and most folks love being infected!

I Took Myself Seriously

Bodacious Woman **Amy Cabellero**

I have been going to the gym somewhat regularly for the past three years. I went because I knew it was good for me. However, I never pushed myself. There was a huge gap in my thinking: How could a gene pool, which gave me chubby knees, ever allow me to build muscle or lose weight? Besides, I thought, everyone who was using weights was training seriously and I would look ridiculous picking up five-pound weights next to them. One day, I just kept my eyes on myself. I rolled up my sleeves to watch my muscles work and concentrated on the sensation of the contractions. I took myself seriously. The frequency to the gym and the weights I used increased. I finally got results that I should've gotten years ago. I still have chubby knees but I don't notice them as much as before!

Infecting Yourself and Others

As you become more bodacious, it's going to be hard to keep the Bodacious Woman you're becoming down. Being bodacious is about being full of life and enjoying the moment. No matter how hard you try (and I suggest you don't try at all!), your enthusiasm is going to leak out. More likely it will ooze. Others are going to notice. They'll wonder what's different about you. They'll be intrigued. More and more, people will be attracted to you. Because, you see, even if they can't put their fingers on what's changed about you, they can tell one thing for sure: You're a good time! You're loving life! And who couldn't use more good times in their lives as they spin 24/7? Being bodacious is contagious, and most folks love being infected!

One of my favorite things to do is go into a greeting-card store to find just the right card for a particular someone and laugh my ass off! (This is an amazing non-aerobic, gluteus maximus exercise.) This activity is especially fun to do with a friend. "Oh, you've *got* to see this one," says one friend to another, which is followed by a moment of silent reading, and then a burst of laughter. **Creating a commotion in a card store is indeed one of life's pleasures. In fact, card store managers should expect and encourage uproarious outbursts.**

This could easily be done by creating *experience zones* throughout the store. For example, there could be a *laugh zone* for humorous cards, a *warm and fuzzy zone* for sentimental cards, and a *quiet zone* for sympathy cards. Just think of the positive vibes bouncing off those four walls!

And I do mean positive. How many cards do you find that say, You hurt me! I hate you! Go away! Okay, so you've searched for one now and then. Why do you think they make those blank cards anyway? The thing is, negative cards just aren't big sellers. But, feel-good cards sure are, enough so that I'd guess card shopping might be enough to replace a therapy session.

I sometimes wonder how cool it would be to have the job of sitting around all day thinking of humorous one-liners and sayings for birthdays, anniversaries, and I love you cards. I imagine this extremely fun group of people gathered around a big conference room table shouting out suggestions and making everyone laugh. "Oh, how about this one!"

Then I think that's probably not how it happens at all. It's more likely just a few people who are suffering over a cup of coffee to come up with, yet again, another creative idea for the fall card collection when their imaginations have been picked dry and they desperately need a trip to Cancun. Well, however, it happens, I'm a Pavlovian consumer captivated by the result. Lead me to the card store and I'm already wagging my tail and feeling happy.

Given my enthusiasm about cards, I'm sure it's no surprise that I love receiving cards as much as giving them. In fact, my estimation of someone skyrockets when they give me a card that perfectly captures something about them, me, and the moment. Often I get a new clue or understanding about the other person, especially how they experience me, and our relationship. See, I told you it was like a therapy session!

A few years ago, a good friend gave me a card that's become one of my favorites. It's not only adorable, it taught me something about the power of being bodacious. Get this picture: On the front of the card is a black-and-white photo of a five-year-old girl with short, curly, dark hair wearing a seersucker bathing suit and sandals. I'm wondering if this is some lost photo from my childhood. Seersucker used to be the fad, you know. So far, pretty cute.

Now add that she's proudly holding up a small fish that she just caught and her mouth is gaping open as she screams in delight. Her whole body, including her chubby little thighs (even at a young age

We'll Make It Work

Bodacious Woman **Diane Bradford**

My daughter broke her ankle one month before her big wedding day. She wrestled with keeping the date; her visions didn't include a bulky cast. Finally she decided: "I'm going to get married on October 14th and that's the way it is!" My response: "If you want to go down that aisle, we'll make it work for you. I don't care what anyone thinks!" We built her a float to sit on and she glided down the aisle like a Rose Bowl Queen, her father sitting by her side to give her away. After the vows, her new husband picked her up, settled her gracefully into his arms and walked back down the aisle as her flower-filled hand shot up in the air victoriously. Come to think of it, we both had a BoMo®!

Asking Questions

Bodacious Woman **Alyson Skinner**

I recently started a beginners' sewing class. (Yes, even Bodacious Women get a domestic urge once in a while.) The instructor has been a professional seamstress and teacher for 20 years. She goes through the motions of how to thread and work the machines, but about every two minutes I ask, "Why? Why not? What would happen if?" She rarely knows the answers to my questions, and while she definitely knows how to sew, she has never wondered herself why or why not or what would happen if. I took it as a bodacious compliment when she exclaimed that in all her years, she has never had a student ask these questions before.

it's good to know it ain't the bod, it's the bodaciousness), is taut with excitement. It is hilarious! Any normal human being can't look at this photo without at least cracking a smile. She just makes you feel good. Inside, the card reads: "Happy Birthday to someone whose excitement is always contagious." Can you see why I absolutely love this card?

I love the idea of being contagious to others! And, honestly, until then, it hadn't occurred to me just how much impact my becoming bodacious was having on other people. I put myself on the bodacious journey because I wanted to take better care of myself and to be empowered. I recognized that most people supported me and liked the new me, for which I was grateful. But, I wasn't living the Bodacious Way for them, I was doing it for me.

Receiving this card enlightened me to the fact that not only is being bodacious highly attractive to others, it is contagious – and in a very good way. Since then, I've noticed the same phenomenon again and again with other Bodacious Women. As soon as they become infected by the bodacious bug, they immediately become a carrier, whether they realize it or not. I guarantee you don't have to be tested! And, I have yet to hear of any complaints.

Join In

If you've read this far, I know one thing for sure. You are serious about becoming a Bodacious Woman! I'm so excited for you! Know that following the Bodacious Woman Mantra will catapult you **toward** coming into your own.

Perhaps you've already started your bodacious journey and need to know you're not crazy or alone. You're not crazy to want to be authentic, empowered, energetic, and happy to be alive. And, you're definitely not alone. As I have shared my bodacious message with

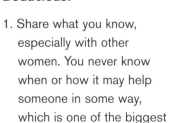

Advice For Becoming Bodacious:

1. Share what you know, especially with other women. You never know when or how it may help someone in some way, which is one of the biggest reasons I think we're all here.

2. Believe it IS possible to live out your dreams. Don't wait another minute to sketch out a plan and embark on your dreams. Don't let a job, a mortgage, or other commitments be your excuse.

3. Ask yourself these three questions and get quiet enough to really listen to your answers: What do I really want? What will it take to get it? Am I willing and able to do what it takes?

   – Bodacious Woman
      Robin Sparks

thousands of women, I've met some amazing women who are resilient, real, and refuse to let life's challenges keep them down. They love using the word *bodacious* and have adopted it into their vocabulary. No doubt their conversations are more lively and memorable! I'm sure others are eavesdropping, just dying to know what they're talking about.

These women have sparked in me the desire to inspire thousands – even millions – of more women to shed their good girl ways and live spirited, gusty, and authentic lives! It would thrill me to no end for women to be calling each other Bodacious Women and recognizing the each other's BoMos®. Being bodacious is indeed contagious, and I want to infect as many women as possible.

I can't do it alone (nor do I want to)! You can bet you're already part of it all. By reading this book and by using the Bodacious Woman Mantra, you are creating a shift in yourself that is already making your world a better place.

Join in the Bodacious Movement

dare to live your

SPIRITED
GUTSY
AUTHENTIC

life

and bring someone with you.

Good for you! But, don't keep a good thing to yourself. Bring others along. And make sure keep filling your tank as well.

Here are three things you gotta do to keep this good thing going:

1. **Seek Out Other Bodacious Women**

   In fact, here's one instance where we must put fashion rules aside. Forget "Less is more." In this case, more is definitely better. Just think of the fun and support you'll have from a group of Bodacious Women. No card store will be safe!

2. **Feed Your Motivation Meter**

   No matter how bodacious you feel right now, there will be moments when you'll wonder where all your spunk went. Maybe on a vacation to the Bahamas without you? Don't worry, it's still there. We all have our ups and downs, but it's the Bodacious Woman who thinks strategically and plans for the emotional ride. She continues to feed her motivation meter.

   Being inspired once isn't enough (myself included). That's why I've created some fun ways to keep you keepin' on. When you go to my website www.GoBodacious.com you'll find them. And, many of them are absolutely free! You just have to go get them. (Hey, I can't do everything for you, nor should I, right?)

   On my website you'll find my fun "How Bodacious Are You?" quiz, all kinds of articles and audio recordings on living bodaciously, and downloadable mini-posters created from the cool graphics in this book that you can post up where ever you want. I also keep you up on the lastest

Support is the Best Defense

Bodacious Woman **Lucy Stribley**

After working with a colleague for several months, I realized that the individual was subtly and not so subtly trying to sabotage my career. After a little data gathering, I found that I was not the only one receiving the same treatment. In response, I met with some of my bodacious female colleagues. During our bodacious mini-summit, we decided the best defense was strong support of each other. Soon after this meeting, the saboteur changed and started actively supporting me. Never underestimate the power of Bodacious Women uniting!

bodacious happenings with my Bodacious Buzz e-zine, e-mails, free teleseminars and more.

Plus, you can get my "Live Like Your Nail Color!" CD mailed to you at no charge! It's my personal gift to you for taking positive action to fill your life with bodacious motivation. This CD is a taste of my Bodacious Women's Club. Each month Club members receive an audio CD in their mailbox (along with a few surprises along the way) filled with tons of fun, practical strategies, and powerful ideas for you to live bodaciously and be the Bodacious Woman you want to be. Membership is less than a monthly manicure, and I mean a cheap manicure at that! To find out all the details go directly to the Club website www.BodaciousWomensClub.com.

bodacious®
•women's club

3. Be Contagious!

Last but not least, infect others and encourage them to become Bodacious Women, too! Actively use the word bodacious and congratulation women on their BoMos®. Share with others the Bodacious Woman Mantra and how it's helped you. Point them to bodacious headquarters at www.GoBodacious.com so together we can inspire them.

The Bodacious Way has already started to take off and will only expand. There are too many Bodacious Women all over the world who want to live like their nail color, who want to live life as an exclamation, rather than an explanation, who dare to be courageously in charge of their lives and lovin' it. In short, they want to be bodacious!

I'm delighted that you're one of them. Just think - you, me and thousands of other Bodacious Women around the world claiming their bodacious selves and being more alive than ever. I truly believe that together we can create a more bodacious world. What a great place to be!

Together we'll create a more **bodacious** *world.*

Exclamation Points

! Bodaciousness doesn't just happen overnight. It's a process. So, keep at it. You'll become the Bodacious Woman you want to be before you know it!

! Seek out other Bodacious Woman with whom you can share your bodacious journey. Just think of the fun, support, and BoMos® you'll have from a group of women striving to live the Bodacious Woman Mantra!

! Feed your motivation meter. We all have our ups and downs, but it's the Bodacious Woman who thinks strategically and plans for the emotional ride. Go to my website www.GoBodacious.com for all kinds of fun ways to help you to keep keepin' on. Make sure to get my new "Live Like Your Nail Color" CD as my gift to you. And, check out how the Bodacious Women's Club can inspire you each month at www.BodaciousWomensClub.com

! Be contagious! Infect others and encourage them to become Bodacious Women, too! Actively use the word bodacious and congratulation women on their BoMos®. Share with others the Bodacious Woman Mantra and how it's helped you. Point them to www.GoBodacious.com so together we can inspire them.

BONUS GIFT
"Live Like Your Nail Color!" CD

Dear Bodacious Woman,

I hope you're feeling more motivated and more bodacious than ever after reading *Bodacious! Woman: Outrageously in Charge of Your Life and Lovin' It!*

To help you keep that lovin' feeling, I have a special gift that I'd like to send you right away. It's my "Live Like Your Nail Color!" CD and it's FREE. There's absolutely no obligation and no strings attached. I even pay the postage. It's my true gift to you.

Are you feeling "Fuzzy Slipper Fabulous"? Do you want to be a "Million Dollar Mamma"? Are you cheering "Let's Wine Down"? Or perhaps you don't put color on your nails and go "au naturel". Not a problem. Wearing them in their natural mode says you dare to be your natural, authentic self.

To get your free "Like Like Your Nail Color!" CD go now to www.BodaciousWomensClub.com. Then, click on the button "I Want My FREE CD" and fill in your mailing address. I'll rush it to you right away.

This CD is a taste of my Bodacious Women's Club. Each month Club members receive an audio CD in their mailbox (along with a few surprises along the way) filled with tons of fun, practical strategies, and powerful ideas for you to live bodaciously and be the Bodacious Woman you want to be. Membership is less than a monthly manicure, and I mean a cheap manicure at that! Find out all the details at www.BodaciousWomensClub.com.

Here's to livin' like your nail color and being courageously in charge of your life and lovin' it!

Cheers,

Mary Foley

Mary Foley

P.S. Inspire your company or organization to be bodacious! Invite me to speak at your next conference, special event, or meeting. Explore the possibilities at my website www.SpeakerMaryFoley.com